Modern Critical Interpretations

Adventures of Huckleberry Finn
Animal Farm
Beloved
Beowulf
Billy Budd, Benito Cereno, Bartleby
    the Scrivener, and Other Tales
The Bluest Eye
The Catcher in the Rye
The Color Purple
Crime and Punishment
The Crucible
Daisy Miller, The Turn of the Screw,
    and Other Tales
David Copperfield
Death of a Salesman
The Divine Comedy
Dubliners
Emma
A Farewell to Arms
Frankenstein
The General Prologue to the
    Canterbury Tales
The Glass Menagerie
The Grapes of Wrath
Great Expectations
The Great Gatsby
Gulliver's Travels
Hamlet
Heart of Darkness
I Know Why the Caged Bird Sings
The Iliad
The Interpretation of Dreams
Invisible Man
Jane Eyre
Julius Caesar
King Lear
Long Day's Journey into Night
Lord Jim
Lord of the Flies
The Lord of the Rings

Macbeth
The Merchant of Venice
The Metamorphosis
A Midsummer Night's Dream
Moby-Dick
My Ántonia
Native Son
1984
The Odyssey
Oedipus Rex
The Old Man and the Sea
Othello
Paradise Lost
The Pardoner's Tale
A Portrait of the Artist as a Young Man
Pride and Prejudice
The Red Badge of Courage
The Rime of the Ancient Mariner
Romeo and Juliet
The Scarlet Letter
A Scholarly Look at the Diary of
    Anne Frank
A Separate Peace
Song of Solomon
The Sonnets
The Sound and the Fury
A Streetcar Named Desire
Sula
The Sun Also Rises
A Tale of Two Cities
The Tales of Poe
The Tempest
Tess of the D'Urbervilles
Their Eyes Were Watching God
To Kill a Mockingbird
Ulysses
Waiting for Godot
Walden
The Waste Land
Wuthering Heights

Modern Critical Interpretations

John Knowles's
A Separate Peace

Edited and with an introduction by
Harold Bloom
Sterling Professor of the Humanities
Yale University

CHELSEA HOUSE PUBLISHERS
Philadelphia

© 2000 by Chelsea House Publishers, a division of
Main Line Book Co.

Introduction © 2000 by Harold Bloom

Printed and bound in the United States of America

10 9 8 7 6 5 4 3 2 1

∞ The paper used in this publication meets the minimum
requirements of the American National Standard for
Permanence of Paper for Printed Library Materials,
Z39.48-1984

Library of Congress Cataloging-in-Publication Data

John Knowles' A separate peace / edited and with an
introduction by Harold Bloom.
        p. cm.— (Modern critical interpretations)
    Includes bibliographical references and index.
    ISBN 0-7910-5663-5 (alk. paper)
    1. Knowles, John, 1926- Separate peace.
2. Preparatory school students in literature.
I. Bloom, Harold. II. Series.
PS3561.N68 S435   1999
813'.54—dc21
                                    99-049120
                                    CIP

Contributing Editors: Thérèse DeAngelis, Tenley Williams

Contents

Editor's Note

My Introduction broods upon the question of how permanent a work *A Separate Peace* may prove to be.

James Ellis reads the novel as a myth of the fall from innocence to experience, while Jay L. Halio strongly defends Knowles's achievement in the genre of the short novel.

The skill of *A Separate Peace*'s narrative is extolled by Ronald Weber, after which Paul Witherington explores the ambiguities that are crucial to the book.

James M. Mellard examines Knowles's use of double perspectives, while Franziska Lynne Greiling meditates upon the novel's thematic of freedom.

An overview of all of Knowles's fiction is provided by James L. McDonald, while the extraordinary, continued reception of *A Separate Peace* is studied by Peter Wolfe.

The personality of Phineas is the concern both of Ian Kennedy and Wiley Lee Umphlett, after which this volume concludes with Gordon E. Slethaug's analysis of the motif of the double in *A Separate Peace*.

Introduction

The paperback of John Knowles's *A Separate Peace* (1960) that I have just employed for rereading the novel, after nearly forty years, is in its ninety-eighth printing. Perpetually popular, *A Separate Peace* nevertheless is a Period Piece, though the period may go on a while longer, as it is most distinctly *the* Phillips Exeter Academy novel of our time, whatever our time turns out to be. Prep school fiction is its own genre, and Knowles certainly composed one of the few authentic classics in that necessarily limited mode.

Knowles has never matched *A Separate Peace*; his other novels and his short stories always seem in the wake of his first book. Finny, the tragic hero, is "too good to be true," as the narrator disarmingly remarks. Gene is more interesting and more culpable, skeptical and finally destructive. If Finny is potentially Natural Man, or Original Virtue, Gene is a quester, never quite able to find himself, and deeply perplexed by his ambivalence towards Finny—an ambivalence that literally cripples a friend, crosses the border into repressed malice, and probably indicates some element, however displaced, of homoeroticism in Gene's stance towards poor Finny, though it would be an error to see that as centering this novel.

If Gene cannot bear Finny's innocence, neither can the mature reader, and so *A Separate Peace*'s peculiar merit is also its weakness: Finny cannot persuade us of his reality. One longs for him to manifest some flaw of spirit that might render him a touch more credible. Perhaps he needs a pinch of Scott Fitzgerald's Gatsby in him, but it is not there.

Unfortunately, Knowles could not resist the temptation of making Finny Christ-like, so that the tree from which he falls intimates the cross. The novel's great virtue, its lightness of style, cannot sustain that heavy symbolism.

1

That Finny's death should be a vicarious atonement for Gene, allowing the guilty friend to make the passage into maturity, fires too heavy a gun for this delicate narrative. Still, Knowles certainly found his audience for *A Separate Peace*, and perhaps the book will endure as long as prep schools do.

JAMES ELLIS

A Separate Peace:
The Fall from Innocence

To read *A Separate Peace* is to discover a novel which is completely satisfactory and yet so provocative that the reader wishes immediately to return to it. John Knowles' achievement is due, I believe, to his having successfully imbued his characters and setting with a symbolism that while informative is never oppressive. Because of this the characters and the setting retain both the vitality of verisimilitude and the psychological tension of symbolism.

What happens in the novel is that Gene Forrester and Phineas, denying the existence of the Second World War as they enjoy the summer peace of Devon School, move gradually to a realization of an uglier adult world—mirrored in the winter and the Naguamsett River—whose central fact is the war. This moving from innocence to adulthood is contained within three sets of interconnected symbols. These three—summer and winter; the Devon River and the Naguamsett River; and peace and war—serve as a backdrop against which the novel is developed, the first of each pair dominating the early novel and giving way to the second only after Gene has discovered the evil of his own heart.

The reader is introduced to the novel by a Gene Forrester who has returned to Devon after an absence of fifteen years, his intention being to visit the two sites which have influenced his life—the tree, from which he

From *English Journal* 53, no. 5 (May 1964). © 1964 National Council of Teachers of English.

shook Finny to the earth, and the First Academy Building, in which Finny was made to realize Gene's act. After viewing these two scenes, a "changed" Gene Forrester walks through the rain, aware now that his victory over his internal ignorance is secure. With this realization Gene tells his story of a Devon summer session and its consequences.

Described as ". . . tremendous, an irate, steely black steeple," the tree is a part of the senior class obstacle course in their preparation for war and is the focal center of the first part of the novel. As the Biblical tree of knowledge it is the means by which Gene will renounce the Eden-like summer peace of Devon and, in so doing, both fall from innocence and at the same time prepare himself for the second world war. As in the fall of Genesis, there is concerning this tree a temptation.

Taunted by Phineas to jump from the tree, Gene says: "I was damned if I'd climb it. The hell with it." Aside from its obvious school boy appropriateness, his remark foreshadows his later fall. Standing high in the tree after surrendering to Finny's dare, Gene hears Finny, who had characterized his initial jump as his contribution to the war effort, reintroduce the war motif, saying: "When they torpedo the troopship, you can't stand around admiring the view. Jump!" As Gene hears these words, he wonders: "What was I doing up here anyway? Why did I let Finny talk me into stupid things like this? Was he getting some kind of hold over me?" Then as Gene jumps, he thinks: "With the sensation that I was throwing my life away, I jumped into space."

What Finny represents in Gene's temptation is the pure spirit of man (mirrored in the boy Finny) answering its need to share the experience of life and innocent love. For Finny the war and the tree, which represents a training ground for the war, are only boyish delights. The reality of war is lost upon him because he is constitutionally pure and incapable of malice. That this is so can be seen from Gene's later statement regarding Finny as a potential soldier. He says:

> They'd get you some place at the front and there'd be a lull in the fighting, and the next thing anyone knew you'd be over with the Germans or the Japs, asking if they'd like to field a baseball team against our side. You'd be sitting in one of their command posts, teaching them English. Yes, you'd get confused and borrow one of their uniforms, and you'd lend them one of yours. Sure, that's just what would happen. You'd get things so scrambled up nobody would know who to fight any more. You'd make a mess, a terrible mess, Finny, out of the war.

The tragedy of the novel ultimately is that Gene is not capable of maintaining the spiritual purity that distinguishes Phineas and so must as he discovers his own savagery betray Phineas.

Once the two jumps have been effected, a bond has been cemented between the two. But as Gene and Finny walk up to the dormitories, Gene forgets that he has, in following Finny, denied the adult rules which regulate human relationships, and lapses back into his concern for authority. Falling into his "West Point stride," he says: "We'd better hurry or we'll be late for dinner." Phineas, however, objects to Gene's having forgotten what is exemplified in the jumping from the tree and trips Gene. After a brief scuffle the two boys resume their walk. Gene, then, acknowledges that he has succumbed to Finny. He says:

> Then Finny trapped me again in his strongest trap, that is, I suddenly became his collaborator. As we walked rapidly along, I abruptly resented the bell and my West Point stride and hurrying and conforming. Finny was right.

To acknowledge visibly his giving up the rules of Devon, Gene now trips Finny, and the two are united in a boy's conspiracy to elude adulthood and its rules.

Gene's Envy

The progress of the novel after this joining of Phineas and Gene is the progress of Gene's growing envy of Finny. Incapable of the spiritual purity of Phineas, Gene finds himself jealous of Finny's ability to flout Devon rules in his quest to enjoy an "unregulated friendliness" with the adult world. Gene says apropos of several incidents involving Finny and the Devon rules:

> I was beginning to see that Phineas could get away with anything. I couldn't help envying him that a little, which was perfectly normal. There was no harm in envying even your best friend a little.

and

> This time he wasn't going to get away with it. I could feel myself becoming unexpectedly excited at that.

And when Finny does evade punishment, Gene thinks:

> He had gotten away with everything. I felt a sudden stab of
> disappointment. That was because I just wanted to see some
> more excitement; that must have been it.

It is during a bicycle trip to the beach on the morning of the day on
which Gene will push Finny from the tree that Finny confides to Gene that
he is his best friend. Gene, however, cannot respond. He says: "I nearly did.
But something held me back. Perhaps I was stopped by that level of feeling,
deeper than thought, which contains the truth." The effect of this trip is to
cause Gene to fail a trigonometry test and thereby to bring his hatred of
Finny into the open. Inventing reasons to explain what exists only in his
projecting it upon Phineas, Gene says as he realized what he thinks is
Finny's plot:

> Then a second realization broke. . . . Finny had deliberately set
> out to wreck my studies. . . . That way he, the great athlete,
> would be way ahead of me. It was all cold trickery, it was all
> calculated, it was all enmity.

Later, just before he will shake Finny from the tree, Gene confronts
Phineas with his suspicions. Finny's surprise at the charge is such that Gene
realizes its falsity. Confronted with the evident truth of Finny's denial,
Gene understands his inferiority to Phineas and his own moral ugliness,
made the more so juxtaposed to Finny's innocence. It is this realization that
prompts his conscious shaking of the tree, which casts Phineas to the earth
and which serves as Gene's initiation into the ignorance and moral
blackness of the human heart.

Returning to the fall session without Phineas, Gene finds that peace
has deserted Devon. And replacing the freedom of his careless summer are
the rules of Devon, to which Gene now gives his allegiance.

Unable to take part in the boyish activities and sports of Devon because
of his guilt, Gene attempts to find anonymity in a dead-end job as assistant
crew manager. But here, confronted with the arrogance of Cliff
Quackenbush (about whom there is an aura of undefined ugliness which
separates him from the other boys), Gene is forced to defend Phineas from
a slighting remark. This fight between Gene and Quackenbush concludes
with their tumbling into the Naguamsett River.

Both the Naguamsett and the Devon flow through the grounds of the
school; but it had been into the Devon, a familiar and bucolic river suggestive

of Eden, that Finny and Gene had jumped from the tree. But after his fall from innocence, Gene experiences a baptism of a different sort as he plunges into the Naguamsett—a saline, marshy, ugly river "governed by unimaginable factors like the Gulf Stream, the Polar Ice Cap, and the moon."

In what Gene says after his fall into the Naguamsett is introduced the latter parts of the paired symbols that were discussed earlier—the winter, the Naguamsett, and the war (fight). Gene says of his fall:

> I had taken a shower to wash off the sticky salt of the Naguamsett River—going into the Devon was like taking a refreshing shower itself, you never had to clean up after it, but the Naguamsett was something else entirely. I had never been in it before; it seemed appropriate that my baptism there had taken place on the first day of this winter session, and that I had been thrown into it, in the middle of a fight.

And just as Gene has gone from the innocence exemplified in the Devon River to the experience of the Naguamsett, so the peaceful Devon River itself, whose course "was determined by some familiar hills a little inland" and which "rose among highland farms and forests," ultimately must succumb to the cosmic force of the world; for it, after passing "at the end of its course through the school grounds," then "threw itself with little spectacle over a small waterfall beside the diving dam, and into the turbid Naguamsett."

Gene's Regeneration

The return of Phineas to Devon signals the rejuvenation and regeneration of Gene. Immediately prior to Finny's return, Gene had discovered in Brinker's announcement of his intention to enlist a chance to close the door on the pain that has haunted him since his crime against Finny. He says of enlistment and its offer to allow him to consecrate himself to the destruction of the war and to his own capacity for evil:

> To enlist. To slam the door impulsively on the past, to shed everything down to my last bit of clothing, to break the pattern of my life—that complex design I had been weaving alone since birth with all its dark threads, its unexplainable symbols set against a conventional background of domestic white and

schoolboy blue, all those tangled strands which required the
dexterity of a virtuoso to keep flowing—I yearned to take giant
military shears to it, snap! bitten off in an instant, and nothing
left in my hands but spools of khaki which could weave only
plain, flat, khaki design, however twisted they might be.

Not that it would be a good life. The war would be
deadly all right. But I was used to finding something deadly in
things that attracted me; there was something deadly lurking in
anything I wanted, anything I loved. And if it wasn't there, as
for example with Phineas, then I put it there myself.

But in the war, there was no question about it at all; it was
there.

But with Phineas' return and Gene's realization that Phineas needs him to
help him maintain his integrity, Gene finds moral purpose and determines to
live out his life at Devon with Finny. He says:

Phineas was shocked at the idea of my leaving. In some way he
needed me. He needed me. I was the least trustworthy person he
had ever met. I knew that; he knew or should know that too. I
had even told him. I had told him. But there was no mistaking the
shield of remoteness in his face and voice. He wanted me around.
The war then passed away from me, and dreams of enlistment
and escape and a clean start lost their meaning for me.

With Gene's resolution, peace returns to Devon and the war is forgotten.

For Phineas, who had even before his fall denied the American
bombing of Central Europe, the war is a make-believe—a rumor started by
various villains who wish to keep the pure spirit of youth enslaved.
Explaining to Gene his vision, Finny points to the roaring twenties "when
they all drank bathtub gin and everybody who was young did just what they
wanted," and then explains that "the preachers and the old ladies and all the
stuffed shirts" stepped in and tried to stop it with Prohibition. But everyone
got drunker so they then arranged the depression to keep "the people who
were young in the thirties in their places." And when they found "they
couldn't use that trick forever," they "cooked up this war fake" for the forties,
the *they* now being "the fat old men who don't want us crowding them out of
their jobs."

What is important in Finny's theory is that it makes of the war an adult
device which curtails the enjoyment of youth and its gifts. To accept the war

is for Finny to accept a fallen world. So persuasive is his own illusion and his own magnetic power that Gene is momentarily caught up in it and can deny the war, the denial, however, being occasioned not so much by Finny's explanation as it is by Gene's "own happiness" in having momentarily evaded the ugliness of the war.

The Phineas-inspired Devon Winter Carnival is the occasion during which Gene is to be paraded in all his Olympic glory, signifying that he, through consecrating himself to Finny's tutelage, has become like Phineas. About this winter carnival and his brilliant decathlon performance, Gene says: ◦

> It wasn't the cider which made me surpass myself, it was this
> liberation we had torn from the gray encroachments of 1943,
> the escape we had concocted, this afternoon of momentary,
> illusory, special and separate peace.

Yet even as this illusion is achieved, a telegram arrives from Leper, an "escapee" from the war, come back to destroy Gene's illusion of withdrawing from the war.

At Leper's home in Vermont, Gene finds himself accused of having been responsible for Finny's fall. Later, after the heat of the accusation has passed, the two boys walk in the snow-covered fields while Leper reveals the horror of the military. As he talks, Gene hears the "frigid trees . . . cracking with the cold." To his ears they sound "like rifles being fired in the distance." This paralleling of the trees (the scene of Gene's fall in particular and nature in general) with the war (and hence the ignorance of human heart, which is responsible for both war and private evil) is given reverberation at Gene's inquisition when Leper describes Gene and Finny as they stood in the tree just before Finny's fall. To Leper they looked "black as death with this fire [the sun] burning all around them; and the rays of the sun were shooting past them, millions of rays shooting past them like—like golden machine-gun fire." Nature then is presented as both damned and damning, with man's death and fall insured by nature's deadly fire and by his own inability to escape the savage within himself.

For Gene, as he listens to Leper, the ugliness of the war finally becomes so forceful that he must run, saying as he does: "I didn't want to hear any more about it. . . . Not now or ever. I didn't care because it had nothing to do with me. And I didn't want to hear any more of it. Ever."

What Gene wants is to return to the world of the winter carnival and his training for the Olympics, his and Phineas' withdrawal from the ugliness of the world. He says:

I wanted to see Phineas, and Phineas only. With him there was no conflict except between athletes, something Greek-inspired and Olympian in which victory would go to whoever was the strongest in body and heart. This was the only conflict he had ever believed in.

Gene's Understanding

The reconciliation of Gene and Finny after Finny's refusal to accept Brinker's "f___ing facts" and his fall provides the culmination of the novel. Questioned by Finny, Gene denies that his pushing of Phineas was personal. Beginning to understand himself, Gene says: "It was just some ignorance inside me, some crazy thing inside me, something blind, that's all." And joined with this realization is Gene's admission that war, despite Phineas, does exist and that it grows out of the ignorance of the human heart. In rejecting Brinker's thesis that wars can be laid to one's parents and their generation, Gene says: ". . . It seemed clear that wars were not made by generations and their special stupidities, but that wars were made instead by something ignorant in the human heart." Gene has discovered that his private evil, which caused him to hurt Phineas, is the same evil—only magnified—that results in war.

Finny alone, Gene now knows, was incapable of malice. Reviewing his relation with Phineas, Gene tells of Finny's way "of sizing up the world with erratic and entirely personal reservations, letting its rocklike facts sift through and be accepted only a little at a time, only as much as he could assimilate without a sense of chaos and loss."

Because of his ability to admit only as much of the ugliness of life as he could assimilate, Phineas was unique. Gene says:

No one else I have ever met could do this. All others at some point found something in themselves pitted violently against something in the world around them. With those of my year this point often came when they grasped the fact of the war. When they began to feel that there was this overwhelmingly hostile thing in the world with them, then the simplicity and unity of their characters broke and they were not the same again.

Phineas alone had escaped this. He possessed an extra vigor, a heightened confidence in himself, a serene capacity for affection which saved him. Nothing as he was growing up at home, nothing at Devon, nothing even about the war had broken his harmonious and natural unity. So at last I had.

It is because of his having known and loved Phineas that Gene can recognize that hatred springs from a greater evil that is within. It is the realization of this that releases him from the hysteria of the war, which now moves from its controlling position off-stage onto the campus of Devon in the form of the parachute riggers.

Unlike his friends who had sought through some building of defenses to ward off the inevitability of evil, Gene has come to see that this enemy never comes from without, but always from within. He knows, moreover, that there is no defense to be built, only an acceptance and purification of oneself through love. Such a love did he share with Phineas in a private gypsy summer. And it is because of the purity of this love that he is able to survive his fall from innocence.

JAY L. HALIO

John Knowles's Short Novels

At a time when best-sellerdom has fostered many overwritten, overpublicized, and often overpraised novels like James Jones's *From Here to Eternity*, William Styron's *Set This House on Fire*, and most recently Philip Roth's *Letting Go*, the problem of how to say much and say it well—in the compass of about two hundred normal-sized pages—has become serious. It has become a challenge to the writer who wishes to go beyond the limitations of the short story in order to develop the full complexities of his theme without at the same time dissipating his art and his energies in much padded or repetitive verbiage. Among younger writers it is therefore heartening to see a few like John Knowles who, taking his cue from *The Sun Also Rises* rather than from *For Whom the Bell Tolls*, has brought back to recent fiction some of the clear craftsmanship and careful handling of form that characterizes our earlier and best fiction in this century.

It is also heartening to see that among the same writers many have shown an unremitting preoccupation with the exploration of the self—a preoccupation, too, of earlier writers, both at home and abroad, but now somewhat relieved of impinging social concerns, though not (which would be a poorer thing) totally divorced from them. The prevailing attitude seems to be that before man can be redeemed back into social life, he must first come to terms with himself, he must first—as has been said so often of

From *Studies in Short Fiction* 1, no. 2 (Winter 1964). © 1964 Newberry College.

American writers—discover who and what he is. That we must look inward and learn to face honestly what we see there and then move onwards or anyway outwards is necessary if in the long run we are to salvage any part of our humanity—if, indeed, humanity is in the future to have any meaning or value. This is the enterprise carried forward in contemporary literature by such novelists as Angus Wilson in England and Saul Bellow at home; and alongside their novels John Knowles has now placed two brilliant pieces of fiction, *A Separate Peace* (1960) and *Morning in Antibes* (1962). His gift is different from theirs as theirs is different from each other, for he speaks with a voice that is at once personal and lyrical in a mode that, with the possible exception of Bellow's *The Victim*, neither of the others has as yet attempted. In his first novel, moreover, Knowles achieves a remarkable success in writing about adolescent life at a large boys' school without falling into any of the smart-wise idiom made fashionable by *The Catcher in the Rye* and ludicrously overworked by its many imitators.

A Separate Peace is the story of a small group of boys growing up at an old New England prep school called Devon during the early years of World War II. The principal characters are the narrator, Gene Forrester, and his roommate, Phineas, or "Finny," who has no surname. As yet but remotely aware of the war in Europe or the Pacific, the boys give themselves up during Devon's first summer session to sports and breaking school rules under the instigations of the indefatigable Finny. It is the last brief experience of carefree life they will know, for most of them will graduate the following June. But within this experience, another kind of war subtly emerges, a struggle between Gene, who is a good student and an able competitor in sports, and Finny, who is the school's champion athlete but poor at studying. Believing Finny's instigations aim at ruining his chances to become valedictorian of their class—and so upset the delicate balance of their respective achievements—Gene awakens to a mistaken sense of deadly enmity between them. (Anyone who has attended such schools will immediately recognize this conflict between intellectual and athletic glory.) Impulsively, Gene causes his roommate to fall from a tree during one of their more spectacular games, and cripples him. This is the central episode of the novel, and the fear which lies behind such destructive hatred is its major theme.

How Gene eventually loses this fear, and so is able to enter that other war without hatred, without the need to kill, is the business of the succeeding episodes. Confession by Gene of deliberate viciousness is alone insufficient release; indeed, far from bringing release, it causes deeper injury to Finny and to himself because of its basic half-truth. Freedom comes only after an honest confrontation of both his own nature and that extension of it represented by Finny, whose loss at the end of the novel he must somehow accept and endure. For if, as the book shows, Finny is unfit for war, and hence unfit for a world engaged in a chronic condition of war, it is because of his fundamental innocence or idealism—his regard for the world not as it is, but as it should be—that renders him unfit. Under Finny's influence, most of the summer of 1942 was, for Gene, just such a world; and it is briefly restored during the following winter when, after convalescing, Phineas returns to Devon. But the existence of this world, and the separate peace this world provides, is doomed. In Finny's fall from the tree Gene has violated, or rather surrendered, his innocence, and he learns that any attempt to regain it, to "become a part of Phineas," is at best a transient experience, at worst a gesture of despair. Nor will either of the twin expedients, escape or evasion, serve him. Escape, as it presents itself to Gene after Finny's second fall, the final crisis in the novel, is rejected as "not so much criminal as meaningless, a lapse into nothing, an escape into nowhere." And evasion— any recourse into the various dodges of sentimentality, such as aggressive arrogance, insensitive factionalism, or self-protective vagueness, as variously portrayed by other boys at Devon—such evasion, Gene comes to realize, is only a mask behind which one does not so much seek reality, as hide from it,. for it is a mask to cover fear. "Only Phineas never was afraid, only Phineas never hated anyone," the book concludes. The essential harmony of his nature could not allow such emotions, and his "choreography of peace" in a world he alone could create and sustain, as for example during Devon's first, only, and illegal "Winter Carnival," is not the dance of this world. His death, coming as it does on the eve of graduation, is, then, for Gene a kind of necessary sacrifice before he can take the next step. And his forgiveness is Gene's way of forgiving himself for what he at last recognizes is "something ignorant in the human heart," the impersonal, blind impulse that caused Finny's fall and that causes war. It is an acceptance, too, the acceptance (as Eliot shows in *Four Quartets*) of a reality which includes ignorance and prepares for humility, without which the next step remains frozen in mid-air.

In *Morning at Antibes*, Knowles prepares to take the next step—or to complete the first—the step that leads to the possibility of human encounter, of real and fruitful meetings with others. But before actually taking this step, he repeats much of what he has already presented in *A Separate Peace*. Perhaps this repetition is necessary for the shape of the novel, which ostensibly is not a continuation of the first (as part of a trilogy, for example) and must tell its own story. But to readers of Knowles's first book, *Morning in Antibes* unavoidably appears as a retelling, in part, of what he has already demonstrated; and so it drags a bit, if only just slightly. The novel opens with the separation of a young couple, Nicholas and Liliane Bodine, after a brief and unhappy marriage. Nick has left Liliane in Paris for the pleasures and transparent lures of the Riviera and for the love he mistakenly hopes to find there; but his unfaithful wife, now deeply troubled and wanting to reconcile, follows him to Juan-les-Pins. It is the summer of 1958, and reflected against this portrait of impending marital dissolution is the mounting struggle of Algeria to free itself from France during the last days of the Fourth Republic: as in *A Separate Peace*, the private and the public war are clearly related. Before reconciliation is possible, however, or even desirable, both Nick and Lili must suffer an agonizing inward look, recognize their self-limitations with neither exaggeration nor minimizing, and with this knowledge of both good and evil in the human heart, discover the means and the will to forgive, and to love.

The first, futile attempt at reconciliation, pushed forward by Liliane, fails badly because it is motivated mainly by a sense of guilt that is as yet too vague to be instructive and by a self-interest that regards her husband primarily as a useful commodity rather than as a fulfilment of her being. Nick, naturally enough, is not interested, even though he allows himself at one point to be trapped into a sexual encounter—which dramatizes for him (as for the reader) the insufficiency of sex, even with so lovely a girl as Liliane, and even in so sex-centered a place as the French Riviera. After this fiasco, Liliane disappears, and a new person enters Nick's life, a young man called Jeannot, whom Nick at first distrusts implicitly: he is an Algerian and all Algerians in France are naturally suspect. But Nick's distrust gradually gives way before Jeannot's gentleness and his profound need to be treated as a human being, even though he is an unemployed Algerian in France during her most stressful period since the War. Nicholas learns a great deal from Jeannot during Liliane's absence, much of it having to do with Jeannot's love for the country which has misprised and misused him. In the midst of Algerian terrorism, which reaches even to the vacation shores of Mediterranean resort towns, Jeannot is no terrorist: like his old father in North Africa, he is forced to give funds to the F.L.N., but that is the extent of his activities. He is troubled by his failure to make good at some profession or trade in France, has left Paris because both terrorism and discrimination have made life impossible for him there, and still loving the country which tries to reject him but at the same time insists he is a part of it—a French citizen with full rights—has come to Antibes. There the French are decent to him; there he is, in his phrase, "well loved," by people who know him. But the Riviera can scarcely help Jeannot to the kind of success that will allow him, a first-born son, to return home without disgrace. Needing a job, but somehow attracted by Nick (whose domestic problems resemble Jeannot's social and political ones), he starts to insinuate himself into Nick's scanty ménage, at one point effecting a momentary but civilized truce between Nick and Lili that is to harbinger their eventual reconciliation.

For it is through Jeannot as much as by his wife's absence—to go on a prolonged cruise with a cynical, degenerate French nobleman—that Nicholas begins to understand what love means and what it demands. Through Jeannot, Nick learns that love begins by valuing (or loving) ourselves justly; only then can we take others at their own just evaluation. Love prevents either party from imposing false valuations upon themselves. In this way Nick's relationship with Jeannot grows and flourishes. Liliane's adultery with Marc De La Croie is an open gesture to show Nick that she has learned to value herself in the way he values her; but in the final resolution of the novel both Nick and Lili realize that this valuation is wrong. Liliane is not so bad as she believes, as her proposed marriage to M. Marc would establish: she is frightened, she confesses—afraid of real love because of the terrifying exertions it repeatedly forces us to make; but in Nick's courage, perhaps, in his willingness to fight, she finds some courage of her own. All this comes out at the end of the novel in her long speech that may be a little too stagey, a little too artificial—as once or twice elsewhere in the novel we feel this to be true—but the essence of what she says is otherwise conveyed, and the speech serves mainly to make it explicit. Significantly, before his reconciliation with Lili occurs, Nicholas and Jeannot part company forever. Learning that the French have killed his father, Jeannot returns home—despite Nick's urgent pleas to come to America with him, to avoid what he cannot make good, what will probably result in his death, too. Graciously, and with deep gratitude, Jeannot refuses Nick's offer of escape or evasion. At the same time, he denies any real courage for what he is about to do; he is simply carrying out the dictates of his heart. "I have to do what I feel there," he says. "Everybody does, it's natural. Everybody does." He still loves France, the country that in its confused, possessive, sadistic way loves him, too; that has enabled him to learn, to get off the hilltop in North Africa and get on the train going somewhere. But it is an impossible love, he sees at last, and now he must go home to help destroy it.

At the end of *Morning in Antibes*, Nick sums up his experience and contrasts it to Jeannot's: "I had come for her. I had not gone away, I had come for her. Not an act of golden courage, not like giving up your life for what lies deeply in your heart; but just a short but definite and irrevocable step. Since I had never walked that way in my life, the first step could only be a short one." In all humility, Nick minimizes the fortitude of his act and the importance of his step. The longest journey begins, after all, with but a single step, however short. It is often the hardest one.

As a second novel, *Morning in Antibes* stands up well against *A Separate Peace*, although readers will doubtless recognize the superior achievement of Knowles's first book. Finny's fall from the tree, while it makes use of old and familiar symbolism, loses none of its power but gains instead by its complete integration within a realistic design. By contrast, Nick's skin-diving episode just before Liliane returns to Juan-les-Pins, though it draws upon equally ancient symbols, parallels too closely Jake Barnes' deep dives off San Sebastion in *The Sun Also Rises*. Here, as in other places, such as a few clipped passages of dialogue, or some detailed descriptions of French cuisine, a purely literary recollection intervenes, detracting from the reader's experience of the presentation and robbing it of some of its felt reality. Nevertheless, in his second novel Knowles retains much of the individual voice mentioned earlier; despite the occasional ventriloquism, it is still there. Moreover, he demonstrates an important development of his theme, and we may well wait for what he has to say next with aroused expectations.

RONALD WEBER

Narrative Method in A Separate Peace

Professor Halio's recent appreciation of the two short novels of John Knowles was especially welcome. Knowles's work, and in particular his fine first novel, *A Separate Peace*, has not yet received the close attention it merits. In a time that has seen high praise for fat, awkwardly-managed novels, he stands out as a precise and economical craftsman. For this alone he demands serious consideration.

Although Professor Halio calls attention to this technical achievement—Knowles, he writes, "has brought back to recent fiction some of the clear craftsmanship and careful handling of form that characterizes our earlier and best fiction in this century"—he is not concerned to illustrate it. He is more interested in examining what he sees as Knowles's second strong point: a thematic concern with the individual's efforts to come to terms with himself as a prior condition to his coming to terms with his society. A reversal of this emphasis—focusing on technique and the relationship of technique to theme—can, I believe, add something to an understanding of Knowles's work. Unlike Professor Halio, however, who gives equal attention to Knowles's second novel, *Morning in Antibes*, I wish to limit my remarks to *A Separate Peace*.

Since the novel deals with young boys in a prep school setting, it inevitably calls to mind *The Catcher in the Rye*. Hoping to capitalize on this

From *Studies in Short Fiction* 3, no. 1 (Fall 1965). © 1965 Newberry College.

similarity, a paperback cover blurb declares it the "best since" *Catcher*. In a different vein, Professor Halio also makes passing reference to Salinger's novel:

> In his first novel . . . Knowles achieves a remarkable success in writing about adolescent life at a large boys' school without falling into any of the smart-wise idiom made fashionable by *The Catcher in the Rye* and ludicrously overworked by its many imitators.

Although the two novels have some obvious similarities, they are fundamentally different books—different in technique, as the quotation suggests, and different in theme. In spite of this, a comparison of *A Separate Peace* with *Catcher*—especially a comparison of the way narrative method relates to theme—offers a useful approach to Knowles's novel.

In both books the narrative is presented from a first-person point of view; both Holden Caulfield and Gene Forrester tell their own stories, stories in which they serve not only as observers but as narrator-agents who stand at the center of the action. Generally, first-person narration gives the reader a heightened sense of immediacy, a sense of close involvement with the life of the novel. This surely is one of the charms of *Catcher* and one of the reasons for its immense popularity. The reader, particularly the young reader, is easily caught up in the narrative and held fast by a voice and an emotional experience he finds intensely familiar. With Knowles's novel, however, this is not the case. While the reader may greatly admire the book, it does not engage him quite as directly or perhaps even as deeply as *Catcher*; throughout it he remains somewhat outside the action and detached from the narrator, observing the life of the novel rather than submerged in it. This difference in reader response, taking place as it does within the framework of first-person, narrator-as-protagonist telling, is, I believe, a highly-calculated effect on Knowles's part. It indicates a sharply different thematic intention, and one that is rooted in a skillful alteration of the conventional method of first-person telling.

Holden Caulfield never comes to an understanding of his experience. He never quite knows that it means; he only feels certain things about it. In the final paragraph of the novel, responding to D.B.'s question about what he now thinks of his experience, he says: "I didn't know what the hell to say. If you want to know the truth, I don't *know* what I think about it." At the end, as throughout the novel, Holden is much more aware of what he feels, in this case a broad sympathy for the people he has described. "About all I know is," he adds, "I sort of *miss* everybody I told about." Gene Forrester, on the other hand, arrives at a clear understanding—a deeply felt knowledge—of the experience he narrates. At the end of the novel he knows, unlike Holden, precisely what he thinks about it.

Understanding demands a measure of distance. We can seldom understand an experience, truly know it, until we are clearly removed from it—removed in time and removed in attitude. Holden achieves such distance only slightly, hence his understanding is slight at best. He tells his story at only a short remove in time from the actual experience of it. It all took place, the reader learns at the start, "around last Christmas." Just as there has been some lapse of time between the experience and the telling, there has also been some shift in Holden's attitude. At the end of the novel, when we again return to the opening perspective, the recuperating Holden now thinks he will apply himself when he returns to school, just as he now sort of misses the people he has told about. In both cases, however, Holden is not sufficiently separated from his experience, either in time or attitude, to admit any real mastery of it.

Holden's relation to the experience of the novel illustrates a major problem of first-person telling. Although the method, by narrowing the sense of distance separating reader, narrator, and fictional experience, gains a quality of immediacy and freshness, it tends for the same reason to prohibit insight or understanding. This latter point has been clearly noted by Brooks and Warren:

> First-person narration tends to shorten the distance between the reader and the fictional character; for instance, the character narrating his own story tends to give us the world strictly in his own terms, in his own feelings and attitudes, and he can scarcely see himself in a large context. He tends to reveal himself rather than to pass judgment upon himself, to give comments about himself, or to analyze himself. Such judgments, comments, and analyses exist in such a story, but they exist by implication, and the reader must formulate them for himself.

Understanding exists in *Catcher*, but not self-understanding for Holden. Because of the intense method of narration, narrowing rather than enlarging the sense of distance in the novel, understanding exists only for the reader, and then only by implication. This situation, as we shall see, is wholly congenial to Salinger's thematic intention; Knowles, however, seeks a different end, and therefore he must somehow modify the effect of his narrative method.

Unlike Holden, Gene Forrester is separated by a broad passage of time from the experience he relates. "I went back to the Devon School not long ago," Gene says in the novel's opening sentence, "and found it looking oddly newer than when I was a student there fifteen years before." That this lapse in time between the experience and the telling has brought understanding is also established early. "Looking back now across fifteen years," Gene says a few paragraphs later, "I could see with great clarity the fear I had lived in. . . ." Although Knowles quickly leaves the distant perspective and turns to immediate scene, he keeps the reader aware that Gene is looking back on the experience with a mature vision. At one point, for example, the distant perspective suddenly opens up at the end of a scene when Gene says: "But in a week I had forgotten that, and I have never since forgotten the dazed look on Finny's face when he thought that on the first day of his return to Devon I was going to desert him." Later, beginning a chapter, Knowles reëstablishes the perspective with a long passage that again looks ahead of the present action:

> That night I made for the first time the kind of journey which later became the monotonous routine of my life: traveling through an unknown countryside from one unknown settlement to another. The next year this became the dominant activity, or rather passivity, of my army career, not fighting, not marching, but this kind of nighttime ricochet; for as it turned out I never got to the war.

The distant point of the narration allows a detachment that permits Gene the mastery of his experience. Even when Knowles gives over the narrative wholly to immediate scene the reader is reminded, sometimes with a phrase, at other times with an entire passage, of the perspective. The war, in addition, serves to create an increased sense of distance, a removal in attitude, within the story. Although the war touches Devon School only slightly—one of the joys of the summer session is that it seems totally removed from the world of war—it cannot be forgotten or ignored for long; it exists not only as an event that stands between the experience of the novel and Gene's telling, but as an event that, at the very moment of the experience, dominates the life of each character. "The war," Gene says in retrospect, "was and is reality for me. I still instinctively live and think in its atmosphere." The anticipation of war forces Gene and his companions into a slight yet significant detachment from their life at Devon—a life that, at

times, seems unimportant and even unreal—and towards an unusual amount of serious, if carefully guarded, reflection. The relation between the fact of war and the atmosphere of detachment or removal in the novel—removal, again, necessary for understanding—can be seen in Phineas' disclosure that, despite his humorous disavowal of the existence of the war, he has been trying for some time to enlist:

> I'll *hate* it *everywhere* if I'm not in this war [he tells Gene]! Why do you think I kept saying there wasn't any war all winter? I was going to keep on saying it until two seconds after I got a letter from Ottawa or Chungking or some place saying, "Yes, you can enlist with us. . . . " Then there would have been a war.

Similarly, the war serves to remove Gene from his immediate experience and to provoke serious self-scrutiny:

> To enlist [he thinks in response to a day spent freeing snowbound trains in a railroad yard as part of the war effort]. To slam the door impulsively on the past, to shed everything down to my last bit of clothing, to break the pattern of my life—that complex design I had been weaving since birth with all its dark threads, its unexplainable symbols set against a conventional background of domestic white and schoolboy blue, all those tangled strands which required the dexterity of a virtuoso to keep flowing—I yearned to take giant military shears to it, snap! bitten off in an instant, and nothing left in my hands but spools of khaki which could weave only a plain, flat, khaki design, however twisted they might be.

The depth of insight revealed in the passage is made possible both by the narrator's removal in time from the experience and by the existence within the experience of the war as a focus of attention outside of him. Finally, the passage suggests how the central dramatic event of the story, Gene's involvement in the injury of Phineas, adds to the atmosphere of detachment in the novel. The injury, which occurs early in the story and underlies the bulk of the narrative, is another force thrusting Gene away from his immediate experience and towards self-scrutiny; as such, it combines with the distant point of the narration and the existence of war to create the broad quality of detachment that makes understanding both possible and plausible.

Gene comes to self-understanding only gradually through a series of dramatic episodes, as we shall see; the final extent of his understanding can, however, be indicated by a passage from the concluding chapter. "I was ready for the war," he says, thinking ahead to his entry into the army, "now that I no longer had any hatred to contribute to it. My fury was gone, I felt it gone, dried up at the course, withered and lifeless." This final awareness contrasts sharply with Holden Caulfield's lack of self-understanding at the end of *Catcher*. While Holden, looking back on his experience, thinks he may be somewhat changed, Gene is certain he is a radically different person. This differing response of the characters to the experience they relate is additionally underscored for the reader by the tone of their narration. In each case, Holden and Gene indicate their relation to their experience as much by how they speak as by what they say and when they say it. Holden's voice, uncertain at times and dogmatic at others, is always exuberant and emotional; it is a voice vividly responsive to the experience of the novel but one that suggests little mastery of it. Gene's voice, on the other hand, is dispassionate, reflective, and controlled; it is, in his own words, a voice from which fury is gone, dried up at its source long before the telling begins. If Holden's voice is that of the restless adolescent groping for an uncertain maturity, Gene's is a voice looking back on adolescence after the hard passage to maturity has been won.

It is clear that Knowles, to return to Professor Halio's phrase, does not fall into the "smart-wise idiom made fashionable" by Salinger's novel. He does not follow in Salinger's wake because of the important variation he works on the method of first-person narration used in *Catcher*. By attempting to maintain a sense of distance within a narrative method that naturally tends to narrow distance, he sacrifices some of the method's freshness to gain depth and insight. In *Catcher* the reader, with Holden, tends to respond to the experience with feeling rather than knowledge; understanding exists for him in the novel only by implication. In *A Separate Peace* the reader, with Gene, remains partially detached from the experience, able to examine and reflect upon it; and understanding can finally take the form of direct statement.

At this point we can begin to see some connection between Knowles's narrative method and his thematic concern. Again, comparison with *Catcher* is useful. Both novels, in a broad and very basic sense, are concerned with the response of the central character to an awareness of evil in the world; they are narratives in which the characters confront, during a concentrated period, part of the reality of life. In face of this reality Holden Caulfield suffers a severe physical and mental breakdown. At the end of the novel, when Holden admits he misses the people he has told about—the assorted phonies who represent the world—the reader is to understand that he now has begun to make some beginning accommodation with that world. Holden of course does not understand this change; it is, as we have said, merely a new feeling, a feeling of missing people he previously despised. Although it is clear that some change has taken place in Holden, it is important to see that it is explained in terms of other people; what must in fact be an inner change—Holden arriving at some peace within himself—is communicated in exterior terms.

In the course of his maturing process, Gene Forrester likewise must confront the fact of evil in the world. But in this case the location of that evil is quite different. At the very beginning of the novel, in a passage quoted earlier, Gene, looking back fifteen years, says he can see with great clarity the "fear" he had lived in at Devon School and that he has succeeded in making his "escape" from. Even now, he adds, he can feel "fear's echo," and this in turn leads him back to the direct experience of the story. The meaning of this experience is to be found in the development of the words *fear* and *escape*—in Gene's growing realization of what they mean as well as what they do not mean.

When his friend and roommate Phineas breaks a Devon swimming record and then refuses to let anyone know about it, Gene is deeply troubled:

> Was he trying to impress me or something? Not tell anybody? When he had broken a school record without a day of practice? I knew he was serious about it, so I didn't tell anybody. Perhaps for that reason his accomplishment took root in my mind and grew rapidly in the darkness where I was forced to hide it.

Later, during an overnight escapade on an oceanside beach, Phineas causes him another moment of uncertainty. Just before the two boys fall asleep, Phineas frankly declares that Gene is his "best pal."

> It was a courageous thing to say [Gene reflects]. Exposing a sincere emotion nakedly like that at the Devon School was the next thing to suicide. I should have told him then that he was my best friend also and rounded off what he had said. I started to; I nearly did. But something held me back. Perhaps I was stopped by that level of feeling, deeper than thought, which contains the truth.

Gene's troubled feelings rise to the level of thought in a following scene during which he comes to the conclusion that Phineas, the school's finest athlete, envies him his academic success. This knowledge instantly shatters any notions he has had of "affection and partnership and sticking by someone and relying on someone absolutely in the jungle of a boys' school." He now sees that Phineas is his rival, not his friend, and this in turn explains his failure to respond properly when Phineas broke the swimming record and when he confessed his friendship. He now sees that he has been envious of Phineas too—envious to the point of complete enmity. Out of the wreck of their friendship this dual rivalry emerges as a saving bit of knowledge:

> I found it [Gene says]. I found a single sustaining thought. The thought was, You and Phineas are even already. You are even in enmity. You are both coldly driving ahead for yourselves alone. You did hate him for breaking that school swimming record, but so what? He hated you for getting an A in every course but one last term.

Their mutual hatred not only explains Gene's inability to respond properly to Phineas, but it relieves him of any further anxiety:

> I felt better. Yes, I sensed it like the sweat of relief when nausea passes away; I felt better. We were even after all, even in enmity. The deadly rivalry was on both sides after all.

Gene's sense of relief, it turns out, is of short duration. When Phineas, in a moment of seriousness, urges him to stick with his studies rather than come along on a campus diversion, Gene suddenly sees he has been wrong—Phineas has never envied him. During a scene immediately following, in which he and Phineas perch in a tree waiting to leap into a river below, Gene is overwhelmed by the implications of this new insight:

> Any fear I had ever had of the tree was nothing beside this. It wasn't my neck, but my understanding which was menaced. He had never been jealous of me for a second. Now I knew that there never was and never could have been any rivalry between us. I was not of the same quality as he. I couldn't stand this.

It is at this moment that he causes Phineas to fall from the tree, an "accident" that cripples him and ends his athletic career. After watching Phineas crash through the branches of the tree and hit the bank, Gene jumps confidently into the river, "every trace of my fear of this forgotten."

It is Phineas' innocence that Gene cannot endure. As long as he can believe Phineas shares his enmity, he can find relief; but with this assurance gone, he stands condemned before himself and must strike out against his tormentor. *Fear*, again, is the key word. Fear in this instance is the emotional response to the discovery of hate, the vast depths of enmity that exist within the human heart. Gene loses his fear and achieves his separate, personal peace only when he acknowledges this fundamental truth. It is a truth that he must first recognize and then accept; he can neither avoid it, as he tries to do in his first encounter with Phineas after the accident, nor flee from it, as he again seeks to do when Leper charges that he always has been a "savage underneath." He can find escape from fear only in the acceptance of its true source and the location of that source. Gene must come to see and endure the truth, as he finally does in a climactic scene just before Phineas dies from a second fall, that his fear is the product not of rivalry nor of circumstance but of "some ignorance inside me, some crazy thing inside me, something blind."

None of Gene's companions at Devon could bring themselves to face this inner source of their fear. When they began to feel this "overwhelmingly hostile thing in the world with them," they looked beyond themselves and felt themselves violently pitted against something in the outer world. When they experienced this "fearful shock" of the "sighting of the enemy," they began an "obsessive labor of defense" and began to parry the menace they thought they saw facing them. They all

> constructed at infinite cost to themselves these Maginot Lines against this enemy they thought they saw across the frontier, this enemy who never attacked that way—if he ever attacked at all; if he was indeed the enemy.

The infinite cost in this case is the loss of self-knowledge. Only Phineas is an exception; only Phineas "never was afraid" because only he "never hated anyone." Phineas alone is free of the awareness of that hostile thing that is to be found not across any battlefield but within the fortress itself. As the archetypal innocent, he must serve as the sacrifice to Gene's maturity. "I was ready for the war," Gene says at the end, "now that I no longer had any hatred to contribute to it. My fury was gone. . . . Phineas had absorbed it and taken it with him, and I was rid of it forever."

Gene Forrester comes to learn that his war, the essential war, is fought out on the battlefield within. Peace comes only when he faces up to this fact. The only escape, the price of peace, is self-awareness. One finds the resolution of Holden Caulfield's war, on the other hand, beyond him, in his relation to society. As Holden flees a corrupt world he is driven increasingly in upon himself, but towards collapse rather than awareness. Salinger presents the hope that is finally raised for him not in terms of self-knowledge but in the ability to move out of himself. It is not, then, awareness that is offered for him so much as a kind of accommodation; he must somehow learn to live, as Mr. Antolini tells him, with what is sickening and corrupt in human behavior. Although this implies facing up to what is corrupt in his own nature, this is not Salinger's emphasis. He seeks to focus the novel outside Holden rather than within him; and for this the conventional method of first-person narration with its tendency to narrow and intensify the story, eliminating the sense of distance vital for the narrator's self-understanding, is admirably suited. Knowles, using a similar but skillfully altered narrative method, develops a very different theme—that awareness, to put it baldly, must precede accommodation, that to look without before having first searched within is tragically to confuse the human condition. To convey his theme Knowles modifies the first-person narrative to create for both narrator and reader an atmosphere of detachment that permits the novel to be focused within Gene, where, he shows, a basic truth of life is to be found.

While the reader may come to feel the experience of *A Separate Peace* somewhat less than that of *Catcher*, he eventually knows it more. While Salinger may give him a stronger sense of life, Knowles provides a clearer statement about life. Although the two novels work towards different ends with different means, they help finally to illustrate, in their separate ways, the close functional relation of meaning and method of telling in carefully-wrought fiction.

PAUL WITHERINGTON

A Separate Peace:
A Study in Structural Ambiguity

The development and resolution of tensions between Gene and Finny provide the well-balanced structure of *A Separate Peace*, as several critics have noted. What has not been appreciated, however, is the ambiguity of the boys' conflict in its several phases, an ambiguity expressed in both character and symbol. The story is not a simple allegory of man's fortunate or unfortunate fall from innocence, or even an extension of that theological debate to the process of growing up, though both of these arguments are in the novel. Rather, Knowles is investigating patterns of society as a whole, patterns consisting of ambiguous tensions between rigidity and flexibility, involvement and isolation, and magic and art. To understand the necessity of a broader interpretation of the novel than has been generally given, one must see that for Knowles opposite emotions and forces only seem to face or move in contrary directions.

The relationship between Finny and Gene is said to be one of primitive innocence confronted with and eventually destroyed by the necessities of civilization. Natural, noble Finny, another of the durable procession of American Adams, is maimed and hounded out of Eden by the hatred he is finally forced to see in his best friend, Gene. On the other hand, Gene's emerging recognition of his guilt in Finny's fall from the tree signals his passage from childhood's innocent play to the responsible ethical concerns of

From *English Journal* 54, no. 9 (December 1965). © 1965 National Council of Teachers of English.

adulthood. Phrased socially rather than theologically, there is a movement toward acceptance of the outside world—that of World War II—and corresponding acceptance of the fact that wars occur not only between nations but between individuals, sometimes even friends, and that the blame in either case can be traced to lack of understanding, an ignorance in the human heart.

One difficulty in such interpretations is that Knowles resists defining innocence and evil and their interaction in simplified, allegoric terms. If there are parallels to Eden, they must surely be ironic, for Finny falls physically without sin whereas Gene falls spiritually without any recognizable physical discomfort. Finny's fall (he falls twice, actually, once from the tree and once on the steps at Devon) seems to represent an awareness of evil that is incompatible with his basic assumptions about unity and goodness; his gradual acceptance of Gene's hostility is accompanied by a physical decline which is strongest at the moments of greatest disillusion. But this awareness of evil remains merely physical in Finny. When asked how he knows that World War II is not real, he says, "Because I've suffered." It appears that nothing is learned after all, that Finny never really understands the world around him; his fall is sad, but nothing more. Gene, on the other hand, seems to endure and even to thrive on his knowledge of evil. His metaphysical fall is, after all, painless, for unlike Claggart in Melville's allegory of good and evil, *Billy Budd*, Gene is untouched by the thrust of mistreated innocence; his moments of mental anguish seem strangely inadequate when compared to those of his classmate, Leper. Greek drama develops in Western literature the notion of suffering as a means to understanding, and American literature is full of innocents who fall from purity only to gain a much more valuable wisdom, but the irony in Knowles is that the sufferer does not understand the nature or purpose of his suffering, and the one who does not suffer both understands and prospers. The world of *A Separate Peace* is not the world of Hawthorne but the inverted, shifting mythos of Kafka, for example, the ambiguous moral atmosphere of "In the Penal Colony."

Apparently complicating matters still further is Finny's announcement near the end of the novel that he has really known there was a war all the time, that his pretending otherwise was his defense against being unable to go to war with his friends. Knowles may have gotten into a structural dilemma here; what seems at first in Finny a genuine misconception of human character, a metaphysical innocence, has become a rationalization, the suppression of an unpleasant fact; illusion becomes delusion, and the reader may conclude that Knowles has lost control of his character, that what started as a semiabstract personification of innocence has come to life as a fully realized character who says that, after all, the grapes really were sour.

The answer to these problems is that Finny is no more of a spiritually pure being that Gene is a spiritually depraved being. Both boys project their inadequacies onto others; Gene's transfer of his own hostility onto Finny is balanced by Finny's notion that wars are contrived by "fat old men" who profit from wartime economy. Moreover, Finny is a breaker of rules, not incidentally but systematically. Gene says, of Devon's rigid system of discipline, "If you broke the rules, then they broke you." Finny's anarchy, however, gives rise to a set of rules just as rigid as the school's and just as imperative; Gene describes Finny's pressure for misbehavior metaphorically: "Like a police car squeezing me to the side of the road, he directed me unwillingly toward the gym and the river." Finny's effort to entice Gene from his studies appears just as conscious as Gene's movement of the tree limb causing Finny's fall.

There is something almost diabolical about Finny's "innocence." His power over people is uncanny; Gene describes it as hypnotic, and it consists of inducing others temporarily to suspend their practical, logical systems of belief to follow his non-logical argument, acted out either verbally or on the playing fields. The answers he gives in class are "often not right but could rarely be branded as wrong," for they presuppose a world in which ordinary standards of judgment are impossible. Finny's pranks themselves—skipping classes and meals, wearing the school tie as a belt, playing poker in the dorm—are actually serious offenses only within the disciplinary framework of a prep school. The audacity is his defense of them which is always disconcerting because it is never relevant, or sometimes too relevant, as when he is being frank about a normally touchy subject. Finny's simplicity, by its very rarity, tends to shock and to threaten the established order of things, to throw ordinary people off balance.

Further ambiguity exists in the imagery of flow which Knowles uses to describe Finny's harmony with others and with his environment. Friendship to Finny is a harmony of equal tensions and movements. Like his idea that everybody always wins at sports, this notion of reciprocal benevolence naively presupposes a level of human interaction superior not only to individual selfishness but also to pressures and events of the actual world. "When you really love something, then it loves you back," he tells Gene, but when Finny confesses his feelings for Gene on the beach, Gene is too embarrassed to answer. Finny cannot understand why people build walls between what they feel and what they let others know they feel; his benevolence, a two-way avenue between friends, is his reason for being. His walk, his play and even his body itself are described as a flow, a harmony within and without, a primitive attunement to natural cycles. The world of graduation, the draft, and adult necessity is oriented differently, however, and Finny's rhythm is broken in his fall into the civilized world: "There was an interruption, brief as a drum beat, in the continuous flow of his walk, as though with each step he forgot for a split-second where he was going." After Finny's second fall, on the stairs, he dies when bone marrow gets in the bloodstream and stops his heart.

Yet Knowles is careful not to oversimplify nor to sentimentalize Finny's stopped flow, the heart ruptured by a violent world. Like the Devon River, that clear, innocent center of summer fun in which the boys play their last summer of childhood, Finny is shut off from natural progress, dammed into isolation and perpetual youth. Below the dam the Naguamsett River, center of winter activity and symbolic setting of Gene's "baptism" into the world of adulthood, is "ugly, saline, fringed with marsh, mud and seaweed," but it does flow into the world-encircling sea to be influenced by the Gulf Stream, the Polar Ice Cap, and the moon; like Gene it, eventually, after some difficulty, involves itself in world movements. The Devon and Finny are relics of some earlier, less complex era, self-sufficient but out of the flow of time, able to give rise and even direction to the stream of mankind, but themselves unable to follow into a mature involvement. There is irony in the fact that Gene's rigid, West Point stride endures, whereas Finny's graceful body breaks so easily; of course Finny risks much more, for his position is supported precariously by shaky illusions. Like Billy Budd's stutter which seems aggravated in the moments when he confronts evil in the world and has no adequate language to express his feelings about it, Finny's flawed flow steadily becomes worse with each new awareness of the hate around him.

Finally, love and hate are themselves ambiguous in *A Separate Peace*, from Gene's first suspicious of an undercurrent of rivalry till the time in the army when he wonders if the "enemy" he killed at Devon was really an enemy at all. Gene is never sure of his relationship with Finny because he—like the reader who sees the action through Gene's eyes—is never sure what Finny represents, whether he is a well-meaning friend who simply resists growing up, a pernicious fraud acting out of spite, or a neurotic who builds protective illusions.

Ambiguity, then, seems to be Knowles' method of showing that people and their emotions must be treated as complex rather than as simple. Good and evil, love and hatred, involvement and isolation, self and selflessness are not always clearly defined nor their values constant. Part of growing up is the recognition that the human condition is a dappled one, that the wrong we feel in things is often only some pattern erected by fear and ignorance, some rigidity that divides life into lifeless compartments. It remains to show how these patterns are fashioned in the novel and what their effects are on the central characters.

All the boys at Devon build barriers against the outside world; "Maginot Lines" Knowles calls them to emphasize their obsolescence and vulnerability. Leper, Devon's introverted biology student, hunts beaver far up the Devon River, detached and unconcerned, masking fear with a mechanistic approach to life symbolized by his movements on skis, those of a "homemade piston engine." His opposite type is Brinker, the class leader, too busy arranging and presiding over school activities to be frightened of the world outside. Like his father, who exploited service in World War I for its social advantages, Brinker treats war as a necessary but inefficient imitation into community leadership, summing it up in his "shortest war poem": "The war/is a bore." Neither case is meant to be typical, for Knowles is concerned with the poles of experience, not its midsection. Leper shows the fallacy of hiding so far from society that the return is a threat to sanity; the fantasy world he fashions turns into a nightmare in boot camp where he begins to have hallucinations in which things are turned "inside out." Brinker is too close to society to preserve any self-identity or to see others as real, separate people, and he is submerged in a kind of public fantasy. The major patterns, of course, are those described in Finny and Gene, ways of approaching the problems posed by growing up and adjusting to civilization, patterns for the two boys respectively of magic and naturalism.

For Finny, life is a continuous effort to control reality by creating comfortable myths about it. War is only make-believe on the fields and rivers of Devon: a game resembling football and soccer is invented and named, for its speed and devastating unpredictability, "blitzball;" snowball fights are staged as military operations; the tree hanging over the Devon River is a torpedoed ship that must be evacuated. But these games which at first seem to have the practical function of preparing boys mentally and physically for war actually become shields against reality, ways of sugarcoating the externals of war by making its participants invulnerable, like playful Olympian deities. Finny is unable to distinguish between playing and fighting, the forms of which seem similar within his romantic, naive frame of reference. Like his theory of reciprocal benevolence, his theory of games is based on the assumption that what *should be* true *can be* once the proper pattern is erected. It is true that Finny is a superb athlete who usually wins any physical contest, and it is also true that Finny often defines winning and losing—the rules of the game itself—during play, but the real basis for Finny's notion that everybody always wins at sports is his idea that the game consists in finding a proper method of play which then makes its outcome irrelevant. His rigidity in this respect is most apparent in a game he plays badly, poker. Following a plan that ought to win, Finny ignores the fact that he actually never does, even when the game is his own weird invention, like a child who asks and keeps asking a question, learning the language by which to frame it and seeming not to hear the answer that is given.

Finny appears essential to Devon's organized defense against war, not only because he directs the boys' last peaceful summer of play and infuses it with ideals of love and equal interaction, but because he seems to have the power to sustain this idyllic atmosphere beyond its natural limits. Described by Gene, Finny is a primitive, god-like priest celebrating the essential unity and indestructibility of man and nature and mediating between the two: "Phineas in exaltation, balancing on one foot on the prow of a canoe like a river god, his raised arms invoking the air to support him, face transfigured, body a complex set of balances and compensations, each muscle aligned in perfection with all the others to maintain this supreme fantasy of achievement, his skin glowing from immersions, his whole body hanging between river and sky as though he had transcended gravity and might by gently pushing upward with his foot glide a little way higher and remain suspended in space, encompassing all the glory of the summer and offering it to the sky." Even after he falls from the tree, Finny preserves this function as priest. His broken body makes winter seem inevitable but only temporary, and his creation of the winter carnival by fiat ["And because it was Finny's idea, it happened as he said"] is an act of magic designed to recreate the harmony of summer. The ritual is begun by burning the *Iliad*, not so much as a protest against war as a magical attempt to destroy war by destroying an early, typical account of it. Standing on a table at the ceremonies, hopping about on his one good leg in protest against war and deformity, Finny tries to represent life as he feels it should be; the others, intoxicated with their desire for earlier, less demanding forms of existence, allow Finny to lead them in this "choreography of peace," suggesting Hart Crane's line in *The Bridge*: "Lie to us—dance us back the tribal morn."

In Finny's universe all things are possible as long as the bulwark of illusion holds; as long as Finny can believe each morning, for example, that his leg has miraculously healed, there is evidence for all magic, not only his but that of a sympathetic universe. When reality does not meet his expectations, though, he is gradually forced into a defensive position. At Gene's "trial" by fellow students, Finny testifies that he believed the tree itself shook him out and tumbled him to the ground. This is more than a defense of Gene, just as the "trial" is more than Gene's; it is Finny's defense of himself, of his notions of reciprocal benevolence and of the inner harmony of all things, and of that supernatural world which sustains these illusions. The evidence convicts him as well as Gene, but—as his second fall shows—Finny cannot adapt to the fact of a Darwinian universe, a world where there are no absolute principles, but only the reality met in experience. The danger of building unsupportable myths like Finny's is shown in Knowles' second novel *Morning in Antibes* (1962); Nick, the central character, in a state of agony at losing his own hold on reality, "spontaneously" composes a poem illustrating his condition:

> The tightrope walker is tired
> Because he must always lean forward
> To weave the rope

This fall comes—as in so many movie cartoons—not when one does the impossible, but when one realizes that he is doing what in fact is impossible. Finny dies when he realizes he has had no magic, that he can no longer, as Knowles puts it, exist "primarily in space." The other boys are propelled forward into the real world by the force of Finny's violent death, for spring inexorably comes in spite of his physical decay, and the correspondence between the priest and the object of his religion is broken,

Finny's imagination moves always from war to play, first grasping the game as a simile for war and then—when the thought of training for something which he cannot use becomes unendurable—playing the game as a substitute for war. The imaginations of the other boys move in opposite directions, from play to war, for that is the way of growing up, recognizing that the patterns of childhood are masks behind which stand the real patterns of life. One day at Devon these different imaginations, facing opposite directions, reach a high moment of dramatic tension in a mock snow war that prefigures Finny's death: "We ended the fight in the only way possible; all of us turned on Phineas. Slowly, with a steadily widening grin, he was driven down beneath a blizzard of snowballs." Afterwards on the way back the gym, Finny remarks that it was a good, funny fight. Gene does not answer; he has for some time had conscious premonitions about things to come, about a turned-inside-out situation where games become real wars: "I didn't trust myself in them, and I didn't trust anyone else. It was as though football players were really bent on crushing the life out of each other, as though boxers were in combat to the death, as though even a tennis ball might turn into a bullet." This is a prelude to the awareness that world wars are but expansions of individual hatred and ignorance and therefore anticlimactic to the anguish of growing up. For Gene the war with Germany and Japan is a simile for his experiences at Devon, less intense because less personal.

The ability to see patterns between world wars and personal wars and between friendly and hostile conflict is to see at once the horrible depravity and the irony of the world where varying and even conflicting experiences often take on the same form. This consciousness of ambiguity, this appreciation of the variety and relativity of human experience, is what Gene learns. His movement, in short, is not toward the primitive, magical effort to control reality in the sense of making it fit preconceived ideas but toward the naturalistic effort to understand reality by relating it to forms of personal experience. As the patterns of experience are realized, they take on meaning, and this meaning itself is a kind of control, not that of the magician but of the artist who finds order and harmony in the structure of things rather than in categorical moral imperatives.

Rejecting Finny's magical view promotes in Gene a new awareness of self and a new self-responsibility. As the compulsive rituals of Finny give way to Gene's nonprescriptive view, and myth is conceived as serving experience rather than dictating it, Gene separates himself from his environment and recognizes in himself the capabilities for idealism and hatred he had formerly projected on the outside world. This emancipation is represented symbolically in Gene's changing relationship with Finny. At first he thinks of himself, rather guiltily, as an extension of Finny, but after becoming an athlete in his own right he sees Finny as smaller, both relatively and absolutely, like memories from childhood, like the tree at Devon which seemed "high as a beanstalk" and yet is scarcely recognizable years later. Finally Gene thinks of himself as including Finny ("Phineas-filled"), and this indicates his maturity; preserving the myth associated with Finny but only so it can serve him as it serves the artist, as a metaphor for experience.

Finny tries to construct a separate peace by explaining away the war as a fraud or by ignoring its content of violence, and Knowles' message is, of course, that this is impossible. Much as Finny's ideal world of changelessness, irresponsibility, and illusion is desirable—and Knowles does present it as desirable—one must eventually abandon it for the world of possibility. Gene's final comment made on his return to Devon years after the major action of the novel, is the key to what he has learned from the tragedy of Finny: "Nothing endures, not a tree, not love, not even a death by violence. Changed, I headed back through the mud. I was drenched; anybody could see it was time to come in out of the rain." Gene frees himself from fear not by hiding from war and the ambiguities of the human heart, not by building barriers between youth and age, but by accepting the inevitability of change and loss. The act of coming in out of the rain, that ancient criterion distinguishing the idealist from the realist, represents the peace Gene finds, the treaty established between what the world should be and what it really is.

JAMES M. MELLARD

Counterpoint and "Double Vision" in A Separate Peace

A Separate Peace, John Knowles's first novel and winner of the first William Faulkner Foundation Award, has become one of the most popular books for literary study in American education since its publication in 1960. The novel is narrated from the point of view of a man looking back over fifteen years at the climactic events of his youth at a New England preparatory school. This retrospective point of view enables Knowles, like Fitzgerald in *The Great Gatsby*, to present a dual perspective of characters, events, symbols, and settings. Akin, in fact, to the movement of Knowles's recent non-fictional *Double Vision* (1965), the direction of the narrative in the novel is toward the protagonist's recognition and acceptance of a puzzling duality, a "double vision," at the very heart of existence. And because of theme and point of view, the demands of symbolism, characterization, and narrative in *A Separate Peace* make counterpoint the most important technique in Knowles's fiction.

Arising naturally from setting, the novel's contrapuntal symbolism operates organically in the development of its theme, the growth to maturity through the loss of adolescent innocence and the acceptance of adult experience. The basic symbolism is the contrast between the peace of the school and the war going on outside, for it provides the objective correlative for the subjective battles fought by the youthful characters as they search for

From *Studies in Short Fiction* 4, no. 1 (Fall 1966). © 1966 Newberry College.

personal fulfillment. It is against the war, therefore, that Gene Forrester, the central and point-of-view character of the novel, directs most of his thoughts. To Gene, "The war was and is reality"; and for much of the novel, it is the hard world of reality, of the war, that Gene, at times only unconsciously, hopes to evade, a desire he manages to fulfill, during most of the final school year, through the intervention of his friend Phineas, or "Finny," as he is usually called. Gene says, for example, that "the war swept over like a wave at the seashore, gathering power and size as it bore on us, overwhelming in its rush, seemingly inescapable, and then at the last moment eluded by a word from Phineas. . . ." Yet the war, like growth and maturity, can hardly be avoided forever, because "one wave is inevitably followed by another even larger and more powerful, when the tide is coming in." So the youths at Devon, and particularly Gene, enjoy their "momentary, illusory, special and separate peace" whenever they can, just as, during Devon's first Summer Session, the faculty relaxed its controls on the boys because they "reminded them of what peace was like."

The fundamental counterpoint between war and peace, reality and illusion, is made more immediate in the symbolic contrast between the "gypsy" summer and the "unromantic" winter. Members of the only summer session in Devon's history, Gene, Phineas and the others make the best of it, managing to break most of the school's rules while still maintaining the faculty's good will, playing at warfare, making up chaotic new games, such as "Blitzball," and forming new clubs, like the "Super Suicide Society of the Summer Session." Supporting the contrast between the reality of the war and the illusions of peace, the opposition between summer and winter is essentially a balancing of the world of fantasy, dream, and desire against the world of fact, even of nightmare and repulsion. As long as the summer lasts, the sense of peace and fulfillment and happiness conquers the encroachments of the war, with its defeats, frustrations and pain: "Bombs in Central Europe were completely unreal to us here, not because we couldn't imagine it . . . but because our place here was too fair for us to accept something like that. . . ." But just as another wave will follow the one eluded, the Winter Session will replace the Summer Session: "It had been the school's first, but this was its one hundred and sixty-third Winter Session, and the forces assembled for it scattered the easygoing summer spirit like so many fallen leaves." At the first Chapel of the new session, Gene thinks how Devon had changed during the summer, how "traditions had been broken, the standards let down, all rules forgotten," but he also realizes that the summer is past, that retribution awaits:

> Ours had been a wayward gypsy music, leading us down all
> kinds of foolish gypsy ways, unforgiven. I was glad of it, I had

almost caught the rhythm of it, the dancing, clicking jangle of it during the summer.

Still it had come to an end, in the last long rays of daylight at the tree, when Phineas fell. It was forced upon me as I sat chilled through the Chapel service, that this probably vindicated the rules of Devon after all, wintery Devon. If you broke the rules, then they broke you. That, I think, was the real point of the sermon on this first morning.

And at this juncture, with school beginning, the summer over, Phineas gone and unlikely to return because of a shattered leg, and the too, too real world of the war reasserting itself, Gene gives himself to the disturbing thought that the "idiosyncratic, leaderless band" of the summer would soon be back under the control of the "official class leaders and politicians." But because the "gypsy days" had intervened and he had absorbed much from Finny, Gene attempts to fight the world alone, a personal battle doomed to failure, but which has momentary triumphs after Finny returns to guide him. The climax of this battle, the "Winter Carnival," is itself a result of the contrast between winter and summer and Gene's desire to restore the spirit of the past summer in the dead of winter. "On this Saturday at Devon," Gene says, "there was going to be no government," and "on this day even the schoolboy egotism of Devon was conjured away." At the Winter Carnival, just before the news of Leper's army desertion, Gene comes closest to regaining the summer place beside his friend Phineas. But this idyllic interlude is followed immediately by Gene's journey through the demonic wintry wasteland of northern New England to see Leper, a trip which reasserts the fact of the war.

Another use of counterpoint and one even more specific than the seasonal symbolism is the antithesis between the two rivers that run through the Devon campus and that make the school itself part of the dualistic symbolism. As the summer connotes peace and dream and fantasy, the Devon River represents goodness, beauty, even purity: "going into the Devon was like taking a refreshing shower itself, you never had to clean up after it." It is associated with the cultivated, the pastoral, the idyllic, with the "familiar hills," the "highland farms and forests we knew." The "turbid" Naguamsett, associated with winter, suggests everything contrary to the spirit of the Devon: it is "ugly, saline, fringed with marsh," and it is "governed by unimaginable factors." But as the war overtakes peace, and winter replaces summer, the highland Devon must drop into the lowland Naguamsett, a vicissitude which suggests once again that youth cannot avoid the responsibilities of maturity. So, if the events of the "gypsy summer" take place beside and in the Devon, the events of the winter must take place beside and in the Naguamsett. And where the central image of the summer is Gene and his "best pal" Phineas leaping together into the Devon, in a gesture of brotherhood, the key image of the winter session is Gene and Quackenbush catapulting into the Naguamsett, "in the middle of a fight."

In addition to the symbolic counterpoint arising from the temporal and physical settings, contrapuntal character relationships control the development of theme and structure. The major character conflict is that which Gene imagines to exist between him and Finny. Like the novel's symbolism, this conflict grows rather naturally from the setting, for a sense of rivalry often prevails in such schools as Devon. Superficially, it is based upon the school's dual emphasis on athletics and scholarship, because Finny is by far the school's best athlete, while Gene is close to being its very best student. Once Gene decides that they are rivals and that Finny has been artfully concealing his ambitions and attempting to wreck his studies, he decides that they are enemies as well, and, like it or not, they "are even in enmity." But the conflict between Finny and Gene goes much deeper than this, for there are essential oppositions in personality. The fundamental contrast is simply that Gene is all too human and heir to all the weaknesses of flesh and spirit, while Finny, at least as Gene sees him most of the time, is little less than a divinity. Thus where Gene is at times morally and ethically shallow, Finny is the epitome of honesty and openness and fidelity. And yet, of the two, Finny is the nonconformist, for his values are generally self-created, although they never seem self-interested. Thus Gene says,

> . . . I noticed something about Finny's own mind, which was such an opposite from mine. It wasn't completely unleashed after all. I noticed that he did abide by certain rules, which he seemed to cast in the form of commandments. "Never say you are five feet nine when you are five feet eight and a half" was the first one I encountered. Another was, "Always say some prayers at night because it might turn out there is a God."

This last "Commandment" is a good illustration of the quality of Finny's mind, for it in no way represents a self-protective covering of his bets; on the contrary, it shows Finny's desire to see the world as it ought to be; hence Gene's memories are of "Phineas losing even in those games he invented, betting always for what *should* win, for what would have been the most brilliant successes of all, if only the cards hadn't betrayed him." Gene, on the other hand, usually played conservatively, aware at all times of percentages, rules, conventions; consequently, to Gene one of the most astounding of

Finny's feats is not so much his breaking a school swimming record without a day of practice, but his unwillingness to have it publicized or even officially recognized, for what Gene values most, at least in the beginning, is conventional and public approval. Thus while Finny has relative values, Gene's values are absolute; where "Finny's life was ruled by inspiration and anarchy," Gene's "was subject to the dictates of [his] own mind, which gave [him] the maneuverability of a strait jacket." And where Finny is the "essence of . . . peace," freedom, courage and selflessness, Gene, until he becomes, as it were, a part of Finny, is swayed by some "ignorance" inside him and trapped by his own guilt and fear and egotism.

Although Knowles insists upon the contrasts between Finny and Gene, he also shows that the two antithetical personalities can, even must, merge into one, just as summer slides into winter, the Devon into the Naguamsett, peace into war. But if these changes seem to be governed by something absolute and unfathomable and yet seem to create something better out of a process that appears undesirable, Gene's transformation also seems to result in a being of greater durability, if not of goodness, one better able to keep his balance in a chaotic world than either the original Gene or Finny. To Gene, Finny is a god, a god of the river, as his name suggests. But, god or man, Finny is not, as Gene tells him, suited for the world as it is, for the war and, thus, for reality. Hence, Phineas, besides his initial contrast to Gene, even points to a strong contrapuntal character symbolism: both the representative of Gene's "fall from innocence" and grace and the means for his deliverance and redemption, in a novel filled with Christian symbols and a theme linked to the concepts of original sin and the fortunate fall, Phineas becomes both Adam and Christ, the "second Adam," in a concentrated, powerful symbolism that is paradoxical, but also traditionally Christian. And, "Phineas-filled" at the novel's conclusion, Gene is enabled to size up the world, like Phineas, "with erratic and entirely personal reservations, letting its rocklike facts sift through and be accepted only a little at a time, only as much as he could assimilate without a sense of chaos and loss."

The uses of counterpoint in symbolism and characterization are important, but they by no means complete *A Separate Peace*. Of equal significance are the contrapuntal devices of plot and structure. There are many actions that have their counteractions in the novel, but the major counterpointed scenes are those that involve Finny's two falls, the markers that determine the three-part structure of the novel. As in symbolism and characterization, the structure of the novel shows a kind of dialectical movement, first revealing the antitheses between the two central figures, then suggesting the "transformation" of one, Gene, into his opposite, and finally portraying, in dramatically convincing ways, the reconciliation of the opposites into one unified, complete and well adjusted personality, who, better than most, can come to terms with the dual attractions of the world.

The climax of part one, at the end of Chapter Four, is the fall of Phineas from the tree beside the Devon River, but it is prepared for by Gene's increasing suspicions and sense of rivalry. Gene's erroneous but nevertheless powerful distrust of Finny begins to emerge when he watches a sunrise at the beach, after Finny had inveigled him to skip school; it culminates when Gene, in a realization that "broke as clearly and bleakly as dawn at the beach," decides that his friend "had deliberately set out to wreck" his studies so that they would not be even. Shortly after, however, at the tree where the "Suicide Society" members test their devotion to the club, Gene recognizes his tremendous spiritual isolation and physical fear, for, although he cannot yet understand why, he realizes that Finny "had never been jealous . . . for a second." So now he realizes more than ever that he "was not of the same quality" as Phineas, a "truth," however, that he cannot abide at all. Moments later, Gene shakes the limb on which they are balancing and causes Finny to fall. The counterpart to this scene of "crime," at the center of which is a ritual test of personal and idiosyncratic values, is the scene of "punishment," the trial that precedes the second fall at the end of Chapter Eleven. The trial reverses the implications of the first fall, for it indicates Gene's progress away from isolation toward social integration.

Just as the scenes preceding the falls are contrasted, the results of the falls are also carefully counterpointed. The major contrast is in the reversal of the influences upon Gene and Phineas: the first fall is far more important to Gene than to Finny, for while it causes physical anguish for Finny, it creates a much greater emotional anguish for Gene. His anguish releases him from fear, but it creates a social guilt and alienation and a corresponding need to identify completely with Phineas, to "become" Phineas, as it were, in order to escape himself. But as Gene grows more and more sure of himself, of his own identity and "real authority and worth," he comes to depend less and less upon Phineas, who was, because of his disability, so dependent upon Gene that he thought of Gene as an "extension of himself." Consequently, the second fall has far greater ramifications for Finny than for Gene. After this accident, Finny is forced to acknowledge the existence of "something blind" in man's character and to accept the fact that Gene caused his original fall because of "some kind of blind impulse." If the ultimate effect of the two falls upon Gene was to make him more capable of existing in the "real" world, their contrary effect upon Finny was simply to destroy him: as Gene had told him long before, Phineas was "too good to be true," so there really could be no place in the world for him, no matter how hard he or Gene might wish it.

Although Phineas is its most memorable character, *A Separate Peace* is

Gene's story, and the point of that story is Gene's growing into maturity and accepting his place in the world. Consequently, the most important scene for Gene, after the falls, is his inevitable but painful recognition of the world's and his own duality. This recognition involves the contrast of his youthful, adolescent, "old" way of viewing the world with a more mature, adult, "new" way. Occurring just after Phineas' accident on the stairs, in the building where "boys come to be made men," this scene is the literal and symbolic aftermath of Finny's rejection of Gene. It is actually the climax of the novel because Gene's emotional rejection of Finny's way of life is more important than Finny's death; it shows Gene taking a midnight walk through the campus and sleeping overnight in the stadium. During his walk, Gene says, "I was trying to cope with something that might be called double vision. I saw the gym in the glow of a couple of outside lights near it and I knew of course that it was the Devon gym which I entered every day. It was and it wasn't. There was something innately strange about it, as though there had always been an inner core to the gym which I had never perceived before, quite different from its generally accepted appearance." This "double vision" is true of all else that he sees; everything has a "significance much deeper and far more real than any" he had noticed before, taking on meanings, "levels of reality," he had never suspected. His first impression is that he himself lacked reality, that he was a "ghost," a "dream," a "figment which had never really touched anything." But his real problem as well as his most pressing need are revealed when he says, "I felt that I was not, never had been and never would be a living part of this overpoweringly solid and deeply meaningful world around me."

After the night's sleep in the stadium and the awakening to a fresh new perspective on existence, however, Gene walks back to the "center of the school," has breakfast, gets a notebook from his room and goes to class, actions that suggest powerfully that he has given up Phineas and the stadium, as it were, for his own identity and the classroom. Only now is he enabled again to face Finny with the truth about his first catastrophe and, shortly afterward, to accept, almost without pain, the fact of Finny's death. And it is only after his becoming aware of a double view of reality that Gene steps over the threshold of maturity, now able to recognize existence for what it is, to accept his own position in the world; and to go to war without fear or hatred.

If Phineas has "absorbed" the worst of Gene and taken it with him, Gene has himself absorbed and taken with him the best of Finny—"a way of sizing up the world." Although Gene can "never agree with either" Brinker's or Finny's view of the world ("It would have been comfortable, but I could not believe it."), at least Finny's way of sizing it up with "erratic and entirely personal reservations" allowed one to maintain a coherent, integrated personality. But the key word here is *personal*—one must remain true to himself, his own identity, fulfill his own possibilities rather than another's. So if Gene can never be as innocent as Phineas or regain their "paradise lost," he can at least measure others, as well as himself, against Phineas as he measured the world against Devon, in that prelapsarian summer of 1942. And if he and the others fall short of Finny's standard, as they must, they will still gain from having reached for it.

FRANZISKA LYNNE GREILING

The Theme of Freedom in A Separate Peace

Phineas, charming, hypnotic Phineas who "didn't know yet that he was unique," couldn't maintain the innocent freedom of the summer celebrated in *A Separate Peace*. The destruction begins with Gene's outburst of anger and is completed by rule-bound, insensitive Brinker. In the May 1964 *English Journal*, James Ellis detailed Knowles' use of Christian themes in "*A Separate Peace*, The Fall from Innocence." The topic of this article will be not innocence but freedom, the Greek theme of *A Separate Peace*.

Knowles makes a number of obvious references to the Greeks: the burning of *The Iliad* to begin the games at the Winter Carnival, the importance of athletics and the Olympics to Phineas, the Grecian sun "sharp and hard" on the frozen new Hampshire landscape when Gene goes to learn about Leper, and in such context, the repeated use of the words "freedom," "harmony," and "unity." All these are fragments from the Greek themes in the book. Knowles is concerned with the implications of certain Greek ideas: the necessity and effects of freedom, and its corollary ideal of arete: the individual's fulfillment of his own excellences—moral, physical, intellectual, and political. In the first half, Phineas reflects these concerns.

Phineas has a love of excellence and fulfills his ability in the discipline of athletics. When Finny understands that Gene must study to satisfy his ability as a scholar, he says:

From *English Journal* 56, no. 9 (December 1967). © 1967 National Council of Teachers of English.

We kid around a lot and everything, but you have to be serious
sometime, about something. If you're really good at
something, I mean if there's nobody or hardly anybody, who's
as good as you are, then you've got to be serious about that.
Don't mess around, for God's sake.

Phineas represents Greek ideas more than Christian in another way. One
of the basic contrasts between the two philosophies is that the Christians
trust in God while the Greeks believed in man. In John 14:6, Jesus says: "I
am the way, the truth, and the life; no man cometh unto the father but by
me." Hippocrates, who took medicine from the care of the gods to
scientific study by man, said: "Life is short, art is long, the occasion instant,
experiment perilous, decision difficult." The contrast emphasizes the
Greek awareness of the limitations and the greatness of man. Finny
represents Greek more than Christian ideas when he respects the
individual, not inviolable rules. He trusts too much, however. Finny lacks
Hippocrates' mature awareness that while there is much to respect in man,
he is vulnerable to time and ignorance.

Phineas' respect for others is one of the reasons he lives successfully
outside the rules. Finny loves freedom because in it, he can create "a flow of
simple, unregulated friendliness . . . and such flows were one of Finny's
reasons for living." Finny's charm and his delight in giving pleasure to others
allow him to lead other people to break the rules. Phineas "considered
authority the necessary evil against which happiness was achieved by
reaction." Finny himself does not need rules to keep him good; he has an
inner harmony, a humanity which allows him to respond with affection and
generosity to even the rule-givers who must punish him. Phineas assumes
that others would be his equals if only they would ignore the rules. He
cannot understand that rules protect individuals from their own and others'
weaknesses. He does not comprehend fear, envy, rage at one's own moral
ugliness, nor the desire for revenge; so he uneasily ignores these in the
individual and in their public manifestation—the war. In Phineas is an
idealism and innocence which protect him from seeing life as it is, but these
also cause him to try to create around him his ideal world. In the novel, the
best and last example of this special ability is Finny's Winter Carnival. Here,
Finny's denial of war, of evil really, is most successful, and the festival has
risen to anarchy and inspiration.

The hard cider began to take charge of us. Or I wonder now
whether it wasn't cider but our own exuberance which
intoxicated us, sent restraint flying, causing Brinker to throw a

football block on the statue of the Headmaster, giving me, as I put on the skis and slid down the small slope and off the miniature ski jump a sensation of soaring flight, of hurtling high and far through space; inspiring Phineas, during one of Chet's Spanish inventions, to climb onto the Prize Table and with only one leg to create a droll dance among the prizes, springing and spinning from one bare space to another, cleanly missing Hazel Brewster's hair, never marring by a misstep the pictures of Betty Grable. Under the influence not I know of the hardest cider but of his own inner joy at life for a moment as it should be, as it was meant to be in his nature, Phineas recaptured that magic gift for existing primarily in space, one foot conceding briefly to gravity its rights before spinning him off again into the air. It was his wildest demonstration of himself, of himself in the kind of world he loved; it was his choreography of peace.

Appropriate to his defensive innocence, Phineas begins the games by burning *The Iliad*. And here is his flaw, Phineas does not fulfill one of the most prized Greek virtues—intellectual excellence. To Phineas, "freedom" is not the opportunity to "Know thyself."

Perhaps his imperfection makes him all the more Greek. Yet Phineas does partake of the combination of moral and physical beauty that Plato described in *The Republic*.

> And the absence of grace, rhythm, harmony is nearly allied to baseness of thought and expression and baseness of character: whereas their presence goes with that moral excellence and self-mastery of which they are the embodiment.

Phineas' physical beauty and personal harmony remind one of two fifth-century Greek sculptures: Myron's Discobolus and Polyclitus' Doryphorus. The body of the Discus Thrower is slender and competent, the face is serene, revealing an inner calm. The agony of violent effort is absent in this disciplined athlete. The Doryphorus depicts an athlete after performance who, like the Discus Thrower, is unmarked by effort. He walks with a unified, flowing movement, and his face reveals a quiet, inner fulfillment. Both statues reflect a Greek idealism and both express a Greek poise: pride without egotism and self-confidence without complacency. Phineas' poise, like that of fifth-century Greece, is vulnerable. As the Greeks feared, the weakness was in man's inadequate knowledge of himself and his world.

During the decline of Greece, the resulting loss of confidence is evident in sculpture. In the Laocoon, heavily muscled figures struggle against inevitable defeat. These subjects have no harmonious relationship with the cosmos. In *A Separate Peace*, Gene destroys Phineas' unity by committing an act which Phineas cannot assimilate into his view of life.

> All others at some point found something in themselves pitted violently against something in the world around them. With those of my year this point often came when they grasped the fact of the war. When they began to feel that there was this overwhelmingly hostile thing in the world with them, then the simplicity and unity of their characters broke and they were not the same again.
>
> Phineas alone had escaped this. He possessed an extra vigor, a heightened confidence in himself, a serene capacity for affection which save him. Nothing as he was growing up at home, nothing at Devon, nothing even about the war had broken his harmonious and natural unity. So at last I had.

Like the figures of the Laocoon, Phineas is unable to survive when he is betrayed. Gene's is the agonized struggle.

At the beginning, Gene thought of himself as Phineas' equal, first in excellence, then in enmity. Discovering Phineas incapable of hatred, Gene has to face his own moral ugliness and then strikes down Phineas for inadvertently revealing it to him. Rules are unnecessary and restricting for Phineas, but Gene has need of the rules, for he lacks the humanity to make the generous response to others. Gene fails the high demands of freedom, accepts himself as evil, and retreats to the rules.

> It was forced on me as I sat chilled through the chapel service, that this probably vindicated the rules of Devon after all, wintry Devon. If you broke the rules, then they broke you.

In despair, Gene considers committing himself to the evil in his nature. Knowles implies that such action would be a form of death for Gene by alluding to the myth of the Greek fates.

> To enlist. To slam the door impulsively on the past, to shed everything down to my last bit of clothing, to break the pattern

of my life—that complex design I had been weaving since birth with all its dark threads, its unexplainable symbols set against a conventional background of domestic white and schoolboy blue, all those tangled strands which required the dexterity of a virtuoso to keep flowing—I yearned to take giant military shears to it, snap! bitten off in an instant; and nothing left in my hands but spools of khaki which could weave only a plain, flat, khaki design, however twisted they might be.

Not that it would be a good life. The war would be deadly all right. But I was used to finding something deadly lurking in anything I wanted, anything I loved. And if it wasn't there as for example with Phineas, then I put it there myself.

But there is more goodness in Gene than he knows. Phineas, in his need, gives Gene the opportunity to do good and unknowingly gives Gene the self-confidence to be free once more. For Gene's act had damaged Phineas' athletic excellence and, worse, threatened the basis for Phineas' humanity; and Phineas uses his remaining strength to deny this loss. He proceeds to recreate his world through Gene's friendship and athletic development. In this experience, Gene, freed now of envy and despair, understands himself and Phineas.

In fulfilling this second gift of freedom Gene achieves a tragic victory. He is the only one in the book to know himself. The demands on his capacity are symbolized by the workout during which Gene escapes old limits to a new and comfortable level of achievement.

After making two circuits of the walk every trace of energy was as usual completely used up, and as I drove myself on all my scattered aches found their usual way to a profound seat of pain in my side. My lungs as usual were fed up with all this work and from now on would only go rackingly through the motions. My knees were boneless again, ready at any minute to let my lower legs telescope up into the thighs. My head felt as though different sections of the cranium were grinding into each other.

Then, for no reason at all, I felt magnificent. It was as though the aches and exhaustion were all imagined, created from nothing in order to keep me from truly exerting myself. Now my body seemed at last to say, "Well, if you must have it, here!" and an accession of strength came flooding through me. Buoyed up, I forgot my usual feeling of routine self-pity when working out, I lost myself, oppressed mind along with aching body; all entanglements were shed, I broke into the clear.

After the fourth circuit, like sitting in a chair, I pulled up in front of Phineas.

"You're not even winded," he said.

"I know."

"You found your rhythm, didn't you, that third time around. Just as you came into that straight part there."

"Yes, right there."

"You've been pretty lazy all along, haven't you?"

"Yes, I guess I have been."

"You didn't even know anything about yourself."

It is Gene, the scholar, who understands that his sin against Phineas was due to an ignorance of his own nature and that war is a manifestation of a general defensive ignorance in mankind. John K. Crabbe wrote,

> In a moment reminiscent of the shooting of the Arab in Camus' *The Stranger*, Gene cripples his friend and sets in motion a chain of events which leads with Hellenic inevitability to Phineas' death.

But unlike the hero of *The Stranger*, Gene redeems his guilt with understanding. So, at the end of the book, Gene more than Phineas embodies the Greek ideal. He has arete; he has unity. Gene has penetrated the appearances which deceive others and made a harmony of his own that is more profound and more stable than Phineas'.

> As pain that cannot forget falls drop by drop upon the heart and in our despite, against our will, comes wisdom to us from the awful grace of God.
>
> AESCHYLUS

JAMES L. McDONALD

The Novels of John Knowles

It may be too early to attempt more than a tentative appraisal of the overall achievement of John Knowles. Certainly one can say that he ranks among the most promising young American novelists; and one can recognize the obvious fact that *A Separate Peace* (winner of the William Faulkner Foundation Award and the Rosenthal Award) has become a small classic among college students and seems likely to last for some time. His other novels, however, have only been noticed in passing: *Morning in Antibes* and *Indian Summer* have not really been analyzed and evaluated. Nor is there any substantial critical commentary on Knowles's work as a whole.

I would like to begin such a commentary; and I propose to do so by placing Knowles, as it were—by relating him to the American literary tradition which I see him working within. He is writing what Lionel Trilling has called "the novel of manners"; and it seems to me that there are affinities between his aesthetic preoccupations and those of Henry James and F. Scott Fitzgerald. An examination of his subjects, themes, and techniques should show this affinity; and I hope that it will also provide a basis for a reasonably sound estimate of Knowles's stature as a novelist.

From the beginning of his career, Knowles—like James and Fitzgerald—has written about manners, about what Trilling defines as "a culture's hum and buzz of implication . . . the whole evanescent context in

From *Arizona Quarterly* (Winter 1967). © 1967 *Arizona Quarterly*.

which its explicit statements are made." In Knowles's first novel, *A Separate Peace* (New York, 1959), the "explicit statements" are the Second World War and its moral effect on American society; the "context" is made up of the precarious situation of American prep-school students who will soon be combatants, and of the moral responses that they, their teachers, and their parents make to this situation.

As many critics have noted, *A Separate Peace* can be viewed as a war novel, drawing its title from Frederic Henry's personal declaration of personal armistice in *A Farewell to Arms*. Knowles's concern, however, is not with the direct confrontation of the obvious realities of the battlefield; rather, it is with the impact of war on the minds and sensibilities of individuals who are not, as yet, immediately involved. The novel examines the cultural upheaval created by the war, and shows how the resulting moral climate affects the thoughts, feelings, attitudes, and actions of Gene Forrester, Phineas, Leper, Brinker, and the others. The novel deals, then, with culture, and with the sensibility of the individual as it is formed by a particular culture; like James and Fitzgerald, Knowles draws the reader's attention to the individual's efforts to adjust to cultural change, and to the quality of his moral responses as he attempts to cope with the disruption of his formerly stable world.

Particularly Jamesian in this novel is Knowles's use of point of view. The narrator, the principal character, is Gene Forrester. On the surface, it appears that he is telling his story honestly, attempting to grapple with his past and forthrightly informing the reader of its significance. Yet, like the narrators of James's "The Liar" or *The Aspern Papers*, for example, Forrester frequently seems either unaware of or deliberately unwilling to acknowledge the moral nature and consequences of his attitudes and actions. There is, then, a discrepancy between Forrester's judgments and the actions and attitudes he is judging. The reader's awareness of this discrepancy is enforced by the dramatic statements of other characters in the novel, especially by the comments of Leper.

Thus the reader's judgments are not always the same as the narrator's; and so the reader is led to question the narrator's motives and interpretations. Should Forrester be taken at his own evaluation? Or is he really, as Leper charges, "a savage underneath" his pose of refined, dispassionate, reflective survivor and recounter of the ordeal?

The complexity—or the ambiguity—of the novel is precisely here, and so is Knowles's debt to James. Neither novelist merely uses his narrator to direct the narrative. Both, instead, use the narrative as the scene and occasion of a complex, dramatic confrontation between the narrator and his past which the reader participates in. For James and Knowles, the aesthetic effect of this type of novel depends on a dramatic interplay between the narrator's judgments and the reader's; and, in this sense, the narrator is the story.

The locale of Knowles's second novel, *Morning in Antibes* (New York, 1962), naturally leads the reader to think of F. Scott Fitzgerald. Knowles's sleek, sparkling Riviera reminds one of the destructive playground evoked in *Tender Is the Night*. The similarity extends to the quality of observation: Dick Diver himself might have described the "very young couple" that Nick Bodine sees early in Knowles's novel: " . . . the girl angelically lovely, tanned and formed for love, the boy like a nearly naked matador." Knowles's concentration on manners also is akin to Fitzgerald's. Both writers keenly perceive "tone, gesture, emphasis, or rhythm . . . the arts of dress or decoration" as signs of cultural trends; and they use these signs to indicate the moral implications of cultural norms and fashions:

> The French bathing suit was invented because aging women discovered that the skin in the middle of the body often remained soft, and that part of the body shapely, after the arms and legs had begun to coarsen and sag. They were all contenders, wives and mothers for twenty years or not; they were still in training for love.

The actual situation and themes of the novel, however, are closer to those of James than to Fitzgerald's. *Morning in Antibes* offers the classic Jamesian situation of the innocent American encountering the complexities of European culture. The thematic lines of the novel follow James's typical pattern: a conflict between American innocence and European experience is drawn. The naïveté and vitality of the American, Nick and his wife Liliane, are juxtaposed to the worldliness and moral sterility of the Europeans, Marc de la Croie and his sister Constance.

The narrative line of the novel revolves around the struggle between these two worlds for the soul of Liliane; and the struggle is drawn in terms of a sharply defined political situation: the rise of De Gaulle in opposition to French Fascism during the Algerian crisis. But the "evanescent context" of manners is all important in this novel. Liliane's rejection of Marc de la Croie is, of course, a stand against his decadent Fascism: she realizes that he has been "dead for fifteen years," and that in him "nothing survives except the wish to kill." But she is also repudiating the affluent, corrupt cultural norms and attitudes that he represents. Her sarcastic denunciation of de la Croie is framed by a contrast between her natural vitality and the cultivated "atmosphere" in which he plunders:

Her face, fragile and tanned, with a certain liquid quality about
her eyes and hair, her face turned radiant then and she said
suddenly: "Do you know, this has been a perfect dinner!
Perfect. I can't tell you. How do you manage to achieve this
atmosphere? So goodbye, Monsieur Marc . . . and remember,
De Gaulle to power! Let me stress, never has there been such
a dinner!" I started with her out of the dining room.

Politically, the novel, then, raises the question "who will rule France?"
But it also asks what moral positions are involved in this struggle for power;
and Knowles tries to define the cultural attitudes which are desirable and
necessary if the individual is to survive and maintain his integrity. It seems to
me that Knowles has advanced beyond the achievement of *A Separate Peace*.
The issues are drawn more precisely; his subject has a greater range: and his
evaluation of the material is much more clear than it was in his first novel.

Knowles's latest book, *Indian Summer* (New York, 1966), is his most
ambitious attempt to establish himself as a novelist of genuine stature. In it,
he takes up the theme which has obsessed so many major American writers—
"the American Dream." And in dealing with this theme, he seems
deliberately to force the reader to think of F. Scott Fitzgerald and *The Great
Gatsby*.

Certain affinities between Cleet Kinsolving, the hero of *Indian
Summer*, and Fitzgerald's Nick Carraway are immediately discernible. Both
encounter the world of the rich, the wealth and luxury, the success and the
good life to which so many Americans aspire. Both act as stewards to the
rich: Nick to Gatsby and the Buchanans; Cleet to the Reardon family. Cleet
helps to oversee a party given by the Reardons; and Knowles inserts a list
which, echoing the "hum and buzz" of our culture and thus presenting its
implications, cannot but recall Nick's memorable list of those who came to
Gatsby's parties:

There were Mr. and Mrs. Hugh G. Harvey and their daughter
Cassie; Charles Crownover, whose play *Maxine* had been a
Broadway success during the wartime season, when any theatre
which opened its doors had been assaulted by people desperate
for a means to spend their money and forget the war; Mrs.
Morgan Seelinger; Parker Evans Sharp, the retired radio
singer; Fred Hatch, soccer coach at Country Day, and his wife,
the librarian; the Craft girls, Ginny and Mary Eleanor; Gloria
Garrison, who was very good fun and always had been; Mrs.
Van Revellon; Cynthia Manning and her half brother, Clay

Gingel, who always entertained at parties, she by singing
"Deep Purple" and he by doing tricks; Pauline Frey; Fred and
Kitty Winkler; the Jesse Gerkinses; "Red" and Phyllis
McKecknie; the news commentator Greg Zahl and his girl
friend; Mrs. Margaret Bitting and her daughter Ula; Georgia's
mother and father; Lynn; business associates of Mr. Reardon,
and so on.

The narrative of *Indian Summer* is constructed on a series of gradual
discoveries about the disintegration of the American Dream. Cleet and
Georgia, Neil Reardon's wife, slowly come to an understanding of the
cultural and moral realities of wealth; they learn what money and privilege
have done to the rich. Their discovery is remarkably close to Nick
Carraway's realization that the Buchanans were "careless people" who
"smashed up things and creatures and then retreated back into their money
or their vast carelessness . . . and let other people clean up the mess they had
made." Cleet encounters the same carelessness, the same ruthlessness. So
does Georgia. She learns that the Reardons "used for their own ends
emotions and deception and generosity and bribery and loyalty and ambition
and philanthropy and willfulness . . ."; she realizes that the Reardons'
behavior is based on "charts and . . . instruments . . . passed on from fortune
to fortune as though these very rich families all belonged to some secret
confraternity, with special totems and rituals and, above all, special rights."
    It is a case of wealth hideously and dangerously misused. Success has
been attained; but the Reardons, like the Buchanans, have lost the American
Dream of greatness, the vision of the ideal, which inspired it:

> It was as though the energy which created the fortune burned
> as fiercely in the new generation as ever, but with no goal now,
> and where it had before pursued the next deal, it pursued a fox
> or a stag, the genius for investment gambling was turned to
> poker, the family tenacity transferred from commerce to
> tennis, the gift for grasping the moment's opportunity shifted
> from finance to tourism, the ability to organize complex
> situations quickly and efficiently passed from the world of
> business into the world of friends and picnics.

The American Dream now exists only as a memory of what once might
have been. Nick Carraway thinks of the "fresh, green breast of the new
world" which had once appeared to the Dutch sailors, of something which

was "for the last time in history . . . commensurate" to man's "capacity for wonder"; and he realizes that the dream has vanished with the past, "somewhere back in that vast obscurity beyond the city, where the dark fields of the republic rolled on under the night." Cleet Kinsolving and Georgia also sense this loss. The American Dream has vanished, and now, "as America started into the second half of the twentieth century," Georgia knows that there is no dream worthy of the dreamer, that "the world had become too mechanized for his [Cleet's] kind of nature, he asked too much of life. . . . What a pity, what a waste, what a tragedy. . . . He was like a beautifully armored warrior facing a tank." Finally, like Nick, Cleet can remember what once might have been: he imagines a magnificent square-rigger sailing down the Connecticut River, "carrying on its stem head a beautiful figure of an angel, its wings flung back against the great oak hull, gliding seraphically above the waters. . . ."

Knowles, however, adds another dimension to Cleet Kinsolving. As Georgia realizes, Cleet is "one of the few remaining heirs to a far older tragedy" than the unfulfilled promise of the American Dream. His face, expression, and impassivity exhibit "the last vestiges and relics of his Indian blood . . . that persistent strain in his nature making him sometimes utterly bewildered by this America today . . . " Cleet is "an alien who however felt in his blood that this was and always has been home"; he is the "aboriginal American, bound and affronted."

As such, then, Cleet is an embodiment of the "Adamic Myth" which so many critics have seen as characteristic of American literature. And, as such, he can be related to the "bound and affronted" heroes of Henry James, struggling honorably for life amidst those forces which stifle it. He stands with Christopher Newman, Isabel Archer, Adam Verver, and Milly Theale; he has taken the advice which Lambert Strether offered to little Bilham:

> " . . . don't forget that you're young—blessedly young; be glad
> of it . . . and live up to it. Live all you can; it's a mistake not to.
> It doesn't so much matter what you do in particular, so long as
> you have your life. If you haven't had that, what *have* you had?"

Cleet's "deepest ambition" is "simply to be a full human man, making the best of himself." His greatest fear is of being "defeated as most people in the world were . . . simply by not really living, eaten by the termites of a half life semilived." He knows that he has "to be closer to the pulse of life, to feel it pound, to be scared and ecstatic and despairing and triumphant by turns." Cleet may not be as eloquent as Strether; but essentially his ideal, and his message, are the same:

" . . . people can't delay their life if they've got any sense, not wait, stall, that's why they've got to make the life they want early and soon, before it's too late. . . . "

Clearly, *Indian Summer* is another step forward for Knowles. He has dared to treat a theme which has been dealt with by some of the masters of American fiction—Cooper, Melville, Twain, James, Dreiser, Fitzgerald, and Faulkner, for example. Few contemporary novelists would be willing to risk the obvious comparisons.

It would be foolish, of course, to claim that Knowles belongs in the select company of Fitzgerald and James, to contend that *Morning in Antibes* and *Indian Summer* are comparable in quality to *Tender Is the Night* and *The Ambassadors*. But I think that he is an enormously promising novelist, and that he has already achieved a genuine stature. He has exhibited the courage to tackle large subjects and significant themes; and he has treated them with taste, understanding, and considerable technical skill. He certainly deserves more attention than he has received up until now.

PETER WOLFE

The Impact of Knowles's A Separate Peace

John Knowles's concern with morality colors all his books. This preoccupation finds its most general expression in a question asked in *Double Vision* (1964), an informal travel journal: "Can man prevail against the bestiality he himself has struggled out of by a supreme effort?" Knowles's novels, instead of attacking the question head-on, go about it indirectly. They ask, first, whether a person can detach himself from his background— his society, his tradition, and the primitive energies that shaped his life.

The question is important because Knowles sees all of modern life shot through with malevolence. The sound the "frigid trees" make during a winter walk in *A Separate Peace* resembles "rifles being fired in the distance"; later, a character likens the rays of the sun to a volley of machine-gun fire. The book cries to be read in the context of original sin: its central event of a character falling from a tree: the snakelike rush of sibilants in "The Super Suicide Society of the Summer Session," an informal daredevil club whose founding leads to the novel's tragedy: an ocean wave that "hissed . . . toward the deep water" after upending a character: the "dead gray waves hissing mordantly along the beach" the next day.

This universal implication in guilt makes good a major premise of Knowles's fiction: that the condition of life is war. *A Separate Peace* describes the private battles of a prep school coterie boiling into the public fury of

From *The University Review* 36, no. 3 (March 1970). © 1970 The Curators of the University of Missouri.

59

World War II. The individual and society are both at war again in Knowles's second novel, *Morning in Antibes* (1962), where the Algerian-French War invades the chic Riviera resort, Côte d'Azur. *Indian Summer* (1966) not only presents the World War II period and its aftermath as a single conflict-ridden epoch; it also describes civilian life as more dangerous than combat.

The Knowles hero, rather than tearing himself from his background, submerges himself in it. According to Knowles, man can only know himself through action; he learns about life by acting on it, not by thinking about it. The action is never collective, and it always involves treachery and physical risk.

A full life to Knowles is one lived on the margins of disaster. Brinker Hadley in *A Separate Peace* and Neil Reardon in *Indian Summer* are both actionists, but since their lives are governed by prudence and not feeling they can never probe the quick of being. In order to touch the spontaneous, irrational core of selfhood, man must act unaided. At this point Knowles's ontology runs into the roadblock of original sin. Whereas the characters in his books who shrink from a bone-to-bone contact with life are labelled either escapists or cowards, the ones who lunge headlong into reality are usually crushed by the reality they discover. That all of Knowles's leading characters smash their closest friendship and also fall sick conveys the danger of a highly charged encounter with life.

This danger increases because of the way they go about the problem of self-being. Instead of struggling out of bestiality, to use Knowles's metaphor from *Double Vision*, they sink back into it. The Knowles hero moves forward by moving backward. *A Separate Peace* mentions "the deep tacit way in which feeling becomes stronger than thought," "that level of feeling, deeper than thought, which contains the truth," and "that deep layer of the mind where all is judged by the five senses and primitive expectation."

Prime being, then, is both sensory and prereflective, a tremor of uncensored energy. By obeying this dark urgency we can unleash a wildness that cuts down everything it its path. Gene Forrester insists that his shaking of his best friend, Phineas, out of a tree was prompted by "some ignorance inside me"; later he says that "wars were made . . . by something ignorant in the human heart." The first movers of our consciousnesses are "ignorant" in that they override reason and order. But unless we give them full rein we can never unroll our energies full force.

A Separate Peace shapes the problem of man's inherent savagery to American culture. In contrast to the characters of D. H. Lawrence, those of Knowles do not discharge their deepest impulses sexually. Instead they retrace the familiar American fictional pattern of immersing themselves in the past. But where Fitzgerald's Gatsby hankers after the glamor of first love and Miller's Willy Loman looks back to the days when salesmanship was adventurous, Knowles's Gene Forrester reaches back much further. He sounds the uncharted seas of our common humanity and in so doing both undoes the work of civilization and reawakens the wild meaninglessness of primitive man.

The novel's setting gives Gene's problem an American emphasis. In *Double Vision*, Knowles discusses the primitive barbarism underlying American life: "The American character is unintegrated, unresolved, a careful Protestant with a savage stirring in his insides, a germ of American wildness thickening in his throat." This elemental threat, Knowles continues, is all the more lethal for being hidden: "American life has an orderly, rather dull and sober surface, but with something berserk stirring in its depths."

Devon School in New Hampshire, "the most beautiful school in New England" and a haven of gentility, sportsmanship, and academic honors, has the same sort of deceptiveness. Its tame surface and schoolboy remoteness from World War II make it an unlikely setting for violence. As he does with the smiling, boyish soldiers who appear in the last chapter of the novel, Knowles uses a prep school setting to show that even innocence and beauty cannot escape the corrosive ooze of evil. (Devon's Field House is called suggestively "The Cage," indicating that bestiality is already in force at the school.) Contributing to the irony established by the disjuncture of cause and effect, or setting and event, is Knowles's quiet, understated style. That violence should leap so suddenly out of Knowles's offhand, conversational cadences sharpens the horror of the violence. (In *Double Vision*, Knowles praises E. M. Forster for his ability to stir his readers without raising his voice.)

The first chapter of *A Separate Peace* shows Gene Forrester returning to Devon fifteen years after the key incident of his life—that of shaking his best friend Phineas out of a tree and shattering his leg. Mingling memory and fear, Gene is not only the archetypal criminal who returns to the scene of his crime or the American fictional hero who retreats into a private past. His return to Devon is purposive, even compulsive. His neglecting to mention his job, his family, or his home suggests that he has none of these things, even though he is past the age of thirty. He relives his act of treachery and the events surrounding it in the hope of recovering the separate peace of the summer of 1942.

Gene interests us chiefly because of his moral ambiguity: whereas he accepts his malevolence, he also resists indulging it at the expense of others. Fear of unleashing his inherent wickedness explains his inertia since Devon's

1942–43 academic year. It also explains his psychological bloc. His first-person narration is laced with self-abuse, special pleading, flawed logic, and evasiveness. As has been suggested, self-exploration is dangerous work, and Gene cannot be blamed if he sometimes cracks under the strain. Out of joint with both himself and his time, he subjects to reason an area of being which is neither rational nor reducible to rational formulas. Although the sum will not add, he has no choice but to try to add the sum if he wants to re-enter the human community.

Like the novel's memoir technique, Gene Forrester's name certifies that *A Separate Peace* is his book. Of the forest, Gene is a primitive, bloodthirsty woodlander; his occasional self-disclosures spell out the urgency of his death-pull: "I was used to finding something deadly lurking in anything I wanted, anything I loved. And if it wasn't there . . . I put it there myself."

The forest has negative associations throughout the book. At one point Gene is accused of undermining his health by "smoking like a forest fire." Elsewhere the forest is equated with the raw icy wilderness stretching from the northern edge of Devon School to "the far unorganized tips of Canada." As it is in Emily Dickinson, summer for Knowles is the time of flowing beauty and intensity of being. The Sommers family are the most vital characters in *Indian Summer*, and the gypsy spree of Gene and Phineas takes place during summer term.

Devon represents the last outpost of civilization to Gene. It wards off the primitive madness encroaching from the great northern forests, and it shields its students from the organized madness of World War II. Devon's 1942 summer term, the first in its history, is giving Gene and Phineas their last reprieve from a war-racked world. At sixteen, the boys, and their classmates are the oldest students at Devon excused from taking both military subjects and preinduction physical exams.

In contrast to this freedom, winter brings loss, unreason, and hardness of heart. Nor is the heartless irrationality equated with Gene's forest background uncommon. His first name universalizes his glacial cruelty. While Phineas is a sport (who happens to excel in sports), Gene is generic, his barbarism deriving from his North American forebears. And the fact that he is a southerner shows how deeply this northern madness has bitten into American life.

The first object of Gene's return visit to Devon is the tree he ousted Phineas from fifteen years before. James Ellis places the tree in a Christian context by calling it "the Biblical tree of knowledge." His interpretation is amply justified by parallels between the novel and orthodox Christianity: everything in the boys' lives changes for the worst after the tree incident, the tree and Christ's crucifix are both wood, the slab of light under the door that announces Phineas's return to Devon is yellow, the color of Judas and betrayal, and Gene chins himself thirty times the next day in the school's gymnasium.

Yet Christian myth fails to exhaust the tree's meaning. Its rootedness in the earth, its riverbank location, and its overarching branches suggest organic life. Lacking a single meaning, the tree stands for reality itself. Knowles develops this powerful inclusiveness by projecting the tree to several levels of being. For the tree not only exists forcibly at more than one dimension; it also brings together different aspects of reality. Over the spectrum of Gene's life, it is by turns an occasion for danger, friendship, betrayal and regret. Remembered as "a huge lone spike dominating the riverbank, forbidding as an artillery piece," the tree is so much "smaller" and "shrunken by age" fifteen years later that Gene has trouble recognizing it.

Nonetheless, as something more than a physical datum, it marks the turning point of Gene's life and colors the rest of his narrative. The furniture in the home of one of his teachers "shot out menacing twigs," and the tree combines metaphorically with both the War and the aboriginal northern frost to create a strong impression of lostness. The tree's combining power, in fact, is as great as its power to halt or cut short. For while it marks the end of the gipsy summer of 1942, it also yokes Gene's past and present lives.

The victim of the tree incident, Phineas, is best summarized by a phrase Knowles uses in *Double Vision* to describe modern Greeks—"a full life lived naturally." Nor is the classical parallel askew. Phineas's name resembles phonetically that of Phidias, who helped set the standard of all-around excellence that marked the golden age of Pericles. (The nickname, "Finny," suggests in another key a throwback to a morality earlier than our Christian-western ethical system.) Although "an extraordinary athlete . . . the best athlete in the school," Finny stands under five feet nine and weighs only a hundred and fifty pounds. His athletic prowess stems not from brawn but from his superb co-ordination and vitality.

Interestingly, the trophies he wins are for gentlemanly conduct. Finny's mastery goes beyond sports. His great gift is the ability to respond clearly and fully: his "unthinking unity of movement" and his favorite expressions, "naturally" and "perfectly okay," express the harmony and interrelatedness of his life. Finny can afford casualness because he gives himself wholly to his undertakings. There is no room for self-consciousness in this dynamic life-mode. There is no room either for formalized rules. Finny's commitment to life overrides the requirements of reason and law, but not out of innate lawlessness. His responses strike so deeply that, while they sometimes make nonsense of conventional morality, they create their own scale of values.

Finny's organicism also sets the style and tempo of the free, unclassifiable summer of 1942. It must be noted that the separate peace Finny and Gene carve out is no idyllic escape from reality. By founding the Super Suicide Society of the Summer Session, membership in which requires a dangerous leap into the Devon River, the boys admit both danger and death into their golden gipsy days. Accordingly, the game of Blitzball, which Finny invents the same summer, includes the bellicosity and treachery that perhaps count as humanity's worst features: "Since we're all enemies, we can and will turn on each other all the time." Nevertheless, the boys rejoice in Blitzball and, while they sustain a fierce level of competition, they manage to avoid injuries.

For opponents do not inflict pain in the world of *A Separate Peace*; the worst menaces dwell not in rivalry but in friendship. Gene and Phineas become best friends, but Gene cannot live with Finny's goodness. Finny's helping Gene overcome fear and his opening his friend to bracing new adventures rouses Gene's worst traits. Man is a hating rather than a loving animal. Franziska Lynne Greiling summarizes deftly the stages leading to Gene's savaging of Finny:

> At the beginning, Gene thought of himself as Phineas' equal, first in excellence, then in enmity. Discovering Phineas incapable of hatred, Gene has to face his own moral ugliness and then strikes down Phineas for inadvertently revealing it to him.

The summary bears close scrutiny. What finally unlooses Gene's venom is Finny's magnanimity. Although Gene's treachery in Chapter Four strikes explosively, incidents in earlier chapters justify it dramatically. Finny's saving Gene at the end of Chapter Two when he nearly falls out of the tree during a mission of the Super Suicide Society compounds his felony. Gene turns the act of loyalty and sacrifice into an occasion for resentment. Instead of being grateful to Finny for saving his life, he blames his friend for tempting him to jump from the tree in the first place.

Chapter Three puts Finny beyond such commonplace resentment. Here he breaks the school's swimming record for the hundred-yard free style but insists that his feat be kept a secret. Chapter Four shows Gene incontestably that Finny has both outclassed and outmanned him. Whereas Gene bases all his human ties on rivalry, he must bolt down the knowledge that Finny is free of envy. This generosity upsets Gene's entire life-mode: "Now I knew that there never was and never could have been any rivalry between us. I was not of the same quality as he."

Of all modern psychoanalytical theories, perhaps Adler's doctrine of masculine protest best explains Gene's malignancy. But even Adler falls short; Gene's cruelty is unconscious and it brings him no prizes. Nothing so simple as worldly success is at stake in the tree incident. For Gene is one of Devon's best students, and he knows that his gifts, although less spectacular than Finny's, are more durable.

Besides having time in his favor, Gene is already Finny's equal: "I was more and more certainly becoming the best student in the school; Phineas was without question the best athlete, so in that way we were even. But while he was a very poor student, I was a pretty good athlete, and when everything was thrown into the scales they would in the end tilt definitely toward me."

By shaking his friend out of the tree, Gene obeys an urge deeper than reason or wounded vanity. But his act of aboriginal madness is empty. The things that happen to him after his treachery demonstrates the pointless waste of violence.

But they do not draw the sting of his violent tendencies. Gene's first reaction to Finny's shattered leg is complex. Since Finny's vitality diminishes Gene, he is glad to be rid of his friend. Finny's confinement in the Infirmary lets Gene become Finny. He calls Finny "noble" and in the next paragraph, after putting on his friend's clothes, says that he feels "like some nobleman." Even the relaxed, supple style in which he writes his memoir fits with his desire to merge with his male ideal.

Ironically, Finny is just as eager as Gene to switch identities. Rather than accusing him of treachery or languishing in self-pity, he tries to recover some of his lost splendor through his friend. Knowles says at one point in the book that a broken bone, once healed, is strongest in the place where the break occurred. The statement applies to Finny's recuperative powers. His athletic career ended, Finny acquires new skills and learns to exist on a new plane while preserving his high standard of personal loyalty.

Everything and nothing have changed. Buoyed up by his heroic ethic, he returns to Devon midway through the winter term and begins training Gene for the 1944 Olympic Games. His training a groundling athlete for a match that will never be held points up the strength of his moral vision. Finny denies the reality of World War II because he knows instinctively that man can only fulfill himself when the ordinary civilized processes of life are reasonably secure.

The two boys institute a routine based on their best gifts: while Finny coaches Gene on the cinderpath and in the gym, Gene helps Finny with his studies. The routine is kinetic. Finny's organizing of the Devon Winter Carnival, like the Blitzball and the Super Suicide Society of the previous summer, represents an acceptance of reality. But the Carnival reflects an even braver commitment to imperfection than the summer romps. It takes no special gifts to make merry in the summer. By celebrating winter, though, Phineas opts for life's harshness as well as its joys; and by choosing the northern reaches of the school as a site for the carnival, he certifies fun and friendship alongside the icy savagery clawing down from the unpeopled North.

Gene ends this regimen because he cannot forgive Phineas for submitting to his brutality. He determines to make his cruelty a counterforce to Phineas's loyalty and courage. After Phineas breaks his leg falling on the slick marble steps of the First Academy Building, Gene follows him to the Infirmary. But instead of showing compassion for his stricken friend, his thoughts turn inward. Astonishingly, his attitude is one of cool self-acceptance. "I couldn't escape a confusing sense of living through all of this before—Phineas in the Infirmary, and myself responsible. I seemed to be less shocked by it now than I had been the first time last August."

    Gene's detachment imparts the final horror to his actions. Yet Phineas can take his worst thrusts. Although he can no longer control his muscular reactions, his mind stays whole. His body breaks before his spirit; he accepts Gene's treachery, and when he dies he has transcended it. Nobody in the book can come near enough to him to kill him. He dies as he had lived—untouched by human baseness. While his broken leg is being set, some of the bone-marrow escapes into his blood-stream and lodges in his heart. In that bone-marrow produces the body's life-giving red corpuscles, Phineas dies from an overplus and a richness of animal vigor.

Gene's barbarism finds another outlet in Elwin "Leper" Lepellier. Although Leper is not so well perceived as Finny, he serves structurally as Finny's foil. Whereas Finny attracts people, Leper is an outsider; and Leper matches Finny's physical breakdown by cracking psychologically. A solitary at school, he is crushed by the tighter discipline and organization practiced by the Army. But the organized madness of the Army, while wrecking his sanity, sharpens his insight. He tells Gene, "You always were a savage underneath," and later in the book he describes the tree episode with a poetic accuracy that lays bare the core of Gene's treachery.

    Yet none of Leper's hearers can understand him. Finny, on the other hand, communicates by bodily movements and is always perfectly understood. Leper's oppositeness to Finny reveals two important things about Gene's savagery: its all-inclusive sweep and its static nature. Although Finny and Leper both grow, Gene is hunkered in his wickedness. In the same way that primitive societies are the least free, he can neither explain nor change himself once he gives in to his primitive drives. Not only does he rake his two best friends; he justifies his butchery: "a mind was clouded and a leg was broken—maybe these should be thought of as minor and inevitable mishaps in the accelerating rush. The air around us was filled with much worse things."

The Leper-Finny doubling motif is but one example of Knowles's fondness for sharp contrast as a structural principle. The author also plays the carefree summer of 1942 against the winter term that follows. He manages his contrast by means of the various associations created by the intervening season, fall.

Finny's fall from the tree by the river, in ending the boys' summer, draws the warmth and light from Devon. Gene notices a chill in the air even before the start of the new term in September: "I knew now it was fall all right." In a telephone call the same day, Phineas tells Gene that he was "completely over the falls" the last time the two boys visited together. Even the elements seem convulsed, as the fight between *Gene Forrester* and Cliff Quacken*bush* by the *river* suggests. The fight also underscores the emptiness of Gene's ravage upon Finny. As soon as Devon's winter term starts without Finny, Gene's status declines. The assistant crew manager's job Gene takes carries no prestige, and his fight with Cliff Quackenbush, one of Devon's most unpopular students, is just as pointless.

The daily character of life at Devon also expresses the darkening shift from summer to winter. The change in mood is observable the first day of winter term: "We had been an idiosyncratic, leaderless band in the summer . . . Now the official class leaders and politicians could be seen taking charge." Gene's murder of the "simple, unregulated friendliness" marking the summer term validates the need for restricting man's freedom. Like that of Hawthorne, Knowles's attitude toward the law is complex. If civilization is to survive, then man's intrinsic savagery must be bridled. Yet any formal legal system will prove unreliable. The members of the older generation described in the book cannot claim any natural or acquired superiority over their sons. They stand to blame for the War and also for the congressional investigating committees the novel attacks indirectly.

Rules and restrictions turn out to be just as poor a standard of civilized conduct as feelings. Knowles introduces the character of Brinker Hadley—a classmate of Finny, Leper, and Gene—to point up the murderous cruelty of the law. Significantly, Brinker does not enter the book until the 1942-43 winter term. He makes the distressing point that man tends to use the law not as a check to man's aggressiveness, but as an outlet. Legalistic, rule-bound, and calculating, Brinker only invokes the law in order to frustrate or to punish. Knowles mentions "his Winter Session efficiency" and later calls him "Brinker and Lawgiver" and "Justice incarnate."

But he also reminds us that although Justice balances the scales of human conduct, she is also blindfolded. Brinker's blind spot is the life of feeling, his fact-ridden life having ruled out compassion. Brinker, who has a large posterior, or butt, presides from the Butt Room, a cellar which is both the dreariest and the lowest site on the Devon campus. Because Gene could not rise to the example set by Phineas, he must pass muster with Brinker's Butt-Room morality. The tree incident not only drives the boys indoors but also downward—both physically and morally:

> The Butt Room was something like a dungeon . . . On the playing fields we looked like innocent extroverts; and in the Butt Room we looked, very strongly, like criminals. The school's policy, in order to discourage smoking, was to make these rooms as depressing as possible.

The structure of *A Separate Peace* includes the same tensions, stresses, and balances. Chapter Seven, the middle chapter of the novel, is dominated by snow, a common symbol for death. Suitably, the big snowfall of Chapter Seven, like the tree incident of Chapter Four, occurs out of season. Chapter Seven also introduces Brinker Hadley and restores Phineas to Devon. As the chapter advances, the thickening snows envelop Gene; by the end of the chapter, they obstruct all of life.

On the day of Phineas's return, two hundred Devon students volunteer to shovel the snow from the tracks of a local railroad yard. The heavy work, the trainful of soldiers that passes by, and the sickly, quarrelsome foreman of the snow removal combine to make this "misbegotten day" an epitome of death. Finny's coming back to school in November, finally, changes Gene's mind about enlisting. With Finny as a roommate, Gene does not need the War as an outlet for his aggressiveness.

Gene's visit to Finny's home in Boston in Chapter Five and his visit to Leper's in Chapter Ten contain enough striking similarities and differences to stand as mutually explanatory. In Chapter Ten Leper, painfully disoriented after his abortive tour of military service, accuses Gene of having deliberately knocked Phineas out of the tree the previous summer. Gene hotly denies the charge and goes on to abuse and then desert Leper during his crisis: "I was the closest person in the world to him now." Chapter Five, curiously, shows Gene confessing the same treachery and Finny defending him to himself.

The two chapters mirror each other nearly perfectly: Gene reverses field completely, and Finny's self-command balances Leper's mental collapse. But Gene's shift in roles from self-accuser to self-defender is flawed. He

shows Leper none of the kindness extended by Finny in Chapter Five, even though his moral situation in chapter Ten is less difficult than Finny's was.

Gene's failure is one of moral escapism. When Leper reveals himself as a misfit in a world where nothing fits with anything else, Gene flees. Leper's description of the ugliness and disjointedness underlying life strikes Gene so hard that he must deny it in order to keep peace with himself: "I didn't want to hear any more of it. Not now or ever. I didn't care because it had nothing to do with me."

Another pair of incidents whose variations clarify theme take place in Chapter Three and Chapter Eleven—the third chapter from the end of the novel. The element of Chapter Three is water: Finny breaks Devon's swimming record for the hundred-yard free style, and then swims for an hour in the ocean. By Chapter Eleven the water has frozen.

After walking out of a mock-serious investigation of the tree incident, Finny falls a second time and breaks his leg on the "unusually hard" white marble steps of the First Academy Building. His flowing energy has been immobilized both by Leper's mental breakdown and the loveless efficiency of the investigation. A fact does not count for Finny until he experiences it personally; his head-on encounters with pain and heartlessness kill his belief in universal harmony, and he can no longer deny the ubiquity of war. His separate peace ended, he merges in the last paragraph of Chapter Eleven with the icy discord that gores all of life:

> The excellent exterior acoustics recorded his rushing steps and the quick rapping of his cane . . . Then these separate sounds collide into the general tumult of his body falling clumsily down the white marble stairs.

The technique of the last chapter tallies well with both the events and the morality it describes. Knowles violates the unity of time by leaping ahead several months to June 1943; he also breaks a basic rule of fictional art by introducing an important character in his last chapter. These discordancies are intentional: a novel about disjointedness should have its components out of joint with each other. Accordingly, *A Separate Peace* extends a chapter after Phineas's death and funeral.

But instead of joining its dramatic and thematic climaxes, the last chapter has a scattering effect. Gene's class at Devon has just been graduated, and the boys are shipping out to various branches of the military. The new character, Brinker Hadley's father, is a World War I veteran whose lofty code of patriotism and service means little to the younger generation.

Mr. Hadley cannot, however, be dismissed as a stale anachronism. His argument implies that he knows something the boys have not yet learned. Combat duty is important to him, not as an immediate goal but as a topic to reminisce about in future years. Could Mr. Hadley be suggesting that maturity contains few pleasures and that only a heroic youth can make up for this emptiness? That the boys overlook this implication means little. The chapter is full of communication failures, including the generation rift Mr. Hadley introduces by visiting Devon.

Another new presence at Devon is the U. S. Army. Devon has donated part of its grounds to a Parachute Riggers' school. Appropriately, the sector of the campus used by the soldiers is the Northern Common. But Knowles pulls a stunning reversal by overturning this fine narrative stroke. For although the Army as the collective embodiment of man's aggressiveness invades Devon from the icy North, man's aggressiveness has already established a stronghold at Devon. Likewise, the convoy of jeeps driving through campus stirs no warlike fervor. The boyish troops are "not very bellicose-looking," and the jeeps do not contain weapons but sewing machines.

The logic of the novel makes eminent sense of this unlikely freight: the sewing machines, which will service parachutes, allude to the novel's central metaphor of falling, and the young soldiers will lunge headlong into violence in the same way as Devon's Class of 1943. By the end of the book, the malevolence uncoiling from man's fallen nature has engulfed all.

Except, strangely, for Gene. His savagery already spent, he has no aggressiveness left for the Navy. Although his country is at war, he is at peace. Yet the armistice is false. A man so askew with his environment enjoys no peace. Gene's lack of purpose not only divides him from his country; it separates him from himself. Divided and subdivided, he is fighting a war just as dangerous as his country's. He has not killed his enemy, as he insists.

His return to Devon in his early thirties and his memoir of Devon's 1942–43 academic year prove that his private struggle has outlasted the public holocaust of World War II. Just as the anvil can break the hammer, the tree incident hurts Gene more than it does Finny. The novel turns on the irony that the separate peace mentioned in its title excludes its most vivid presence—its narrator. Gene's fall 1957 visit to Devon fixes the limits of his fallen life. His self-inventory is either a preparation for life or a statement of withdrawal. But the question of whether he can convert his apartness into a new start goes beyond the boundaries of the novel.

IAN KENNEDY

Dual Perspective Narrative and the Character of Phineas in A Separate Peace

In the best available study of John Knowles's narrative method in *A Separate Peace*, Ronald Weber compares the novel to Salinger's *The Catcher in the Rye* in order to show how Knowles overcomes the limitations of conventional first-person narration. *The Catcher in the Rye*, he says, "illustrates a major problem of first-person telling. Although the method, by narrowing the sense of distance separating reader, narrator, and fictional experience, gains a quality of immediacy and freshness, it tends for the same reason to prohibit insight or understanding." And he suggests that Knowles has counteracted this tendency by separating the narrator from his narrative by such a long period of time—fifteen years—that Gene is endued with a detachment that enables him to understand and, therefore, to master the experiences he narrates. Weber concedes that this leads, in turn, to a loss of the intense immediacy that characterizes Salinger's novel, but claims that "While Salinger may give [the reader] a stronger sense of life, Knowles provides a clearer statement about life."

To suggest, however, that the author who uses a first-person narrator must choose between a character who is too close to the events narrated to interpret them reliably, and one who is too distant to convey their freshness and vitality, is to deny that one can eat one's cake and have it too; and this is the trick that Knowles pulls off so effectively. *A Separate Peace* is narrated by

From *Studies in Short Fiction* 11, no. 4 (Fall 1974). © 1974 Newberry College.

two Gene Forresters, one of whom conveys the actions, feelings, and thoughts of the moment, while the other looks back on that turmoil from a distance of fifteen years and provides intelligent and illuminating comments. Gene the boy is too close to his own experiences to understand them properly, and Gene the man is too removed to express effectively the vitality that characterizes adolescence, but between them they succeed in dissolving the limitations of conventional first-person narration. Although it is true that this method is not conventional, Knowles is not, however, breaking new ground; for after numerous explorations and experiments in first-person narrative, Dickens adopted this method of dual perspective in his telling of *Great Expectations*, in which there can be found much the same balanced oscillation between the narrations of Pip the boy and the commentary of Mr. Pip the man.

In *A Separate Peace*, just as in *Great Expectations*, the shift from one narrative perspective to another is rarely obvious, and so the distinct jump that occurs on page 6 of Knowles's novel is the exception rather than the rule. But perhaps because it is so distinct, this example provides a clear illustration of the difference between the two narrative voices. Gene the man says, "The tree was not only stripped by the cold season, it seemed weary from age, enfeebled, dry," and nine lines later Gene the boy describes it as "tremendous, an irate, steely black steeple beside the river." Thereafter, the distinction between Gene's two narrative voices becomes more blurred, but it is, nevertheless, quite evident on such occasions as, for example, his description of the recognition that Finny's heart was "a den of lonely, selfish ambition." Indeed, for several pages Gene the boy attributes to Phineas characteristics that Gene the adult knows to be entirely absent from his personality, and it is only when the adult voice chooses to reveal to us the absolute falsity of these misconceptions that we discover, as Gene did himself, that Finny is incapable of harboring evil thoughts and feelings towards others. We are deliberately kept unaware of this recognition in order that we can share the intensity of Gene's misguided feelings, and so the boy's voice, which possesses the power of evoking the immediate actuality of an experience, is the exclusive narrator of this section of the story, handing over to the adult only when it becomes important that we understand correctly the significance of what has been happening.

In general, it is the boy's voice that narrates what happens in the novel, and the man's voice that interprets and conceptualizes these events. Sometimes, however, as in the incidence just discussed, the younger Gene also provides us with his interpretations of the actions, thoughts, and feelings of the characters, and when he does so we must be aware of the unreliability of his opinions. Usually, Knowles structures the narrative so that we are misled by the boy's misconceptions only for as long as seems necessary to express the actuality of his thoughts and feelings, and then the course of events, or the adult voice, reveals to us that this adolescent interpretation is false. For example, when Mrs. Patch-Withers discovers at the headmaster's tea that Phineas is using the school tie as a belt, Gene says, "This time he wasn't going to get away with it. I could feel myself becoming unexpectedly excited at that." But then, of course, Finny does get away with it, and Gene tells us, "I felt a sudden stab of disappointment. That was because I just wanted to see some more excitement; that must have been it," a simplistic explanation that both the adult Gene and, retrospectively, the reader know to be an inadequate interpretation of a complex emotional reaction composed of admiration, envy, disappointment, and latent hatred. Again, when Gene comments on Finny's sensational performance in blitzball, it is clear that although he does not understand the nature of his own reaction, the reader and Gene's older self are meant to recognize it as another indication of his developing resentment of his roommate. "What difference did it make? It was just a game. It was good that Finny could shine at it. He could also shine at many other things, with people for instance, the others in our dormitory, the faculty; in fact, if you stopped to think about it, Finny could shine with everyone, he attracted everyone he met. I was glad of that too. Naturally. He was my roommate and my best friend." Moreover, the fact that this is the voice of the boy narrator is emphasized by the obvious difference in tone of the next paragraph, the narrator of which is clearly the adult: "Everyone has a moment in history which belongs to him. . . . For me, this moment—four years is a moment in history—was the war. The war was and is reality for me."

There are occasions, however, when the adult narrator does not later intervene to rectify young Gene's misconceptions, nor does the course of events serve to reveal the unreliability of his comments, and these are the instances when as readers we must be most careful not to accept Gene's interpretations without first scrutinizing them closely. This is particularly true of comments about Phineas. The short novel is primarily about Gene; but since Finny is the catalyst for Gene's developing personality, one must understand Phineas to understand the novel. With the exception of Peter Wolfe, commentators have been content to regard Finny as a static character, naive and romantic, who embodies all innocence, youthfulness, and purity, who cannot survive a collision with evil and violence, and who therefore denies the reality of war and is inevitably crushed by the adult, civilized, real, nasty world. This view accepts at face value such comments of young Gene as that which begins Chapter 11: "I wanted to see Phineas, and Phineas only. With him there was no conflict except between athletes, something Greek-inspired and Olympian in which victory would go to whoever was the strongest in body and heart. This was the only conflict he had ever believed in." But Gene is at this point suffering from the shock of Leper's madness, and so, to counteract that violent reality, he idealizes Phineas and invests him with a dignity and order, in contrast to Leper's savage chaos, which he does not really possess. And this should be evident from the next sentence in the text: "When I got back I found him in the middle of a snowball fight." Nor is this even an ordered snowball fight, since Finny organizes sides only so that he can turn on his original allies, doublecross his new allies, and so utterly confound all loyalties that "We ended the fight in the only way possible; all of us turned on Phineas."

The snowball fight is important for two reasons. First, because it provides an example, other than the Winter Carnival, of Phineas's celebration of winter—Peter Wolfe has written: "By celebrating winter . . . Phineas opts for life's harshness as well as its joys." And second, because it exemplifies, as does blitzball, Finny's attitude to sports. Gene tells us that his friend's attitude is "'You always win at sports,'" and goes on to add, "This 'you' was collective. Everyone always won at sports. When you played a game you won, in the same way as when you sat down to a meal you ate it. It inevitably and naturally followed. Finny never permitted himself to realize that when you won they lost. That would have destroyed the perfect beauty which was sport. Nothing bad ever happened in sports; they were the absolute good." But this reflection belongs to Gene the boy; it has been formed "As we drifted through the summer," and may not, therefore, be reliable. In fact, Finny's behavior at sports suggests that it is only partially true. Neither in blitzball nor the snowball fight is there anything tangible to be won or lost. There is no goal at which the players can arrive, nor can one team in any way defeat another since both activities are anarchic, based only on "reverses and deceptions," betrayal and treachery. Finny excels at blitzball, but he is delighted to lose, in so far as anyone loses, in the snowball fight, just as "he couldn't ask for anything better" when Gene "jumped on top of him, my knees on his chest" on the way back from the fatal tree. We never see Finny engaged in a sport in which some are clearly victorious and some as clearly defeated. All his awards are for good sportsmanship rather than for being the victor in this sport or that. It therefore seems that, as far as Phineas is concerned, there is no goal in sports except the sheer enjoyment of the activity itself; just to participate is to win, and since everyone can participate no one need ever lose.

Nor is it only with reference to sports that we may see Finny to represent a denial of the need that most people feel to divide life into such opposing categories as win and lose, good and evil, fantasy and reality, truth

and illusion, self and other. As Paul Witherington has pointed out, "His walk, his play, and even his body itself are described as a flow, a harmony within and without, a primitive attunement to natural cycles." Gene, on the other hand, describes his own life as "all those tangled strands which required the dexterity of a virtuoso to keep flowing"; but when, in his running, he suddenly finds his rhythm, breaks into the clear, arrives where Finny has always been, he says, "all entanglements were shed" as mind and body become one and he learns what it is to be an integrated personality. This above all is what Finny is, an integrated personality; just as "peace is indivisible," so is Phineas, and this means that he transcends the divisive categorizations that Gene, like most of us, attempts to impose on an indivisible universe. Not only is Finny frequently described in terms of flow, he is characterized as being possessed of extraordinary honesty, "simple, shocking self-acceptance," "uninterrupted, emphatic unity of strength," and great loyalty. All these attributes suggest that integrity, in the fullest meaning of the word, is the keystone of Phineas's character, for even his loyalty is comprehensive: "Finny had tremendous loyalty to the class, as he did to any group he belonged to, beginning with him and me and radiating outward past the limits of humanity towards spirits and clouds and the stars." And again, "He was too loyal to anything connected with himself—his roommate, his dormitory, his class, his school, outward in vastly expanded circles of loyalty until I couldn't imagine who would be excluded."

This loyalty, however, is only one expression of Finny's perception of the universe as an integrated and indivisible unity. From this perception comes his desire to celebrate winter as well as summer; his ability, after his accident, to think of Gene "as an extension of himself," and to transfer to him the athletic abilities that he is now incapable of exercising; his idea that "when they discovered the circle"—the universal symbol of completeness, wholeness, integrity—"they created sports"; his assertion that "when you really love something then it loves you back, in whatever way it has to love"; and his realization that war is a violation of sanity. Leper's madness is a confirmation of Finny's assertion that "the whole world is on a Funny Farm now" because the world is engaged in breaking in pieces the natural integrity of life, and Finny is able to recognize this because he has fallen victim to that "something ignorant in the human heart" which has "broken his harmonious and natural unity." Indeed, it is perhaps precisely because he knows what war is really like that Finny denies its existence, both to protect his own sanity— Leper goes mad when he meets the inverted disorder that is war—and to shelter his friends for as long as possible from its violent ravages. Nor is this possibility contradicted by Finny's revelation that he has all along been attempting to enlist in some branch, any branch, of the service. His intense loyalty compels him to do so, but Gene is, of course, absolutely correct in his recognition that this loyalty could never be limited only to Phineas's allies, but would naturally extend to the enemy as well.

For much of the novel Gene seems to regard Finny's personality as full of contradictions: "a student who combined a calm ignorance of the rules with a winning urge to be good, who seemed to love the school truly and deeply, and never more than when he was breaking the regulations, a model boy who was most comfortable in the truant's corner." But Gene's development throughout the course of the novel includes a gradual acquisition of understanding which culminates in his recognition of Phineas's "way of sizing up the world with erratic and entirely personal reservations, letting its rocklike facts sift through and be accepted only a little at a time, only as much as he could assimilate without a sense of chaos and loss." Finny realizes that facts are not everything, and that to attempt to reduce reality to a collection of facts, to accept facts as equivalent to reality, as Brinker Hadley does, is to accept a chaotic part in place of an ordered whole and hence to suffer "a sense of chaos and loss." Phineas may often seem to contradict himself, but to such an accusation there is Whitman's reply:

> Do I contradict myself?
> Very well then I contradict myself,
> (I am large, I contain multitudes).
>
> "Song of Myself."

It need not necessarily be the case, therefore, that Finny represents a way of looking at life that is so limited, so idealistic, so ignorant of actuality, that contact with reality inevitably shatters it. Instead, he is perhaps possessed of a transcendent clarity of perception that is capable of taking a larger view of life than is normal, and dies only because he is eventually outgunned by the forces that limit, reduce, and fragment the comprehensive integrity of existence.

It is, however, only possible to entertain such a view of Phineas's character and role in the novel if one first recognizes that some of the interpretations that we have of his actions, his feelings, and his thoughts derive from the unreliable commentary of Gene the boy. In order to overcome the limitations of conventional first-person narration, Knowles has divided the narrator's function between two versions of the same person, and there are, as one would expect, considerable differences in perception and understanding between the seventeen-year-old boy who conveys the immediacy of the experiences he narrates and the thirty-two-year-old man whose interpretations of those experiences provide the basis for our understanding of the novella. It is important, therefore, that when the boy narrator does comment on the significance of the action, we exercise greater than usual skepticism before we accept the validity of his opinions.

WILEY LEE UMPHLETT

The Neo-Romantic Encounter

If by the term *romantic* we mean to imply the state of being or condition that emphasizes individual achievement and freedom of persona expression, then the term *neo-romantic*, at least for the purpose of this study, is a necessary one to apply to those fictional heroes of contemporary literature who, like their antecedents, are romantics at heart, but because of the kind of world in which they find themselves are denied the freedom to express themselves naturally in the truly romantic sense of individual achievement.

Pervading "The Eighty-Yard Run" is this kind of neo-romantic sensibility that controls the meaning and atmosphere of much contemporary fiction. Christian Darling has a deep yearning for his past and a more meaningful life, but his symbolic "run" at the end of the story suggests his sense of loss and frustration as to how he may retrieve his lost world.

The neo-romantic hero, then, is a character who inherently knows what he wants in life—usually personal identity and a sense of achievement, but his inability to perceive or evaluate the significance of his actions frustrates his every move to regain his former, idyllic state. Even the domain of the game and the "great, good place" of the forest (nature) no longer hold the meaning they once did; in fact, in most cases they are no longer available to him.

Most neo-romantic types of the sporting myth appear as has-beens.

From *The Sporting Myth and the American Experience*. © 1975 by Associated University Presses.

Divorced from their former athletic identities, they endure a kind of death in life. But an interesting variation of this figure is that of the athlete who dies young, in that through dying in his prime he retains his state of innocence and contributes identity and significance to the character he is inevitably paired with. Significantly, it is the death of the character who lacks self-awareness that results in his spiritual brother's becoming self-knowledgeable. The paradox of the athletic figure as dying athlete or anti-hero is exemplary of the tendency in recent fiction to move from mythic toward ironic modes of expression. But, as Northrop Frye has pointed out, controlled use of irony can also suggest mythic dimensions, as we shall see in certain of the following representative examples of the neo-romantic sensibility.

Both John Knowles in *A Separate Peace* and Mark Harris in *Bang the Drum Slowly* make use of the dying-athlete theme to stress the worth of the personal identity. In both works, the relationship of two major characters is played off in such a way that the pattern of encounter projects a growth in self-knowledge for one of the major characters. In both works, too, the paradox of the athlete's dying young reinforces the meaning. The tone of these novels is neo-romantic in that the major characters are concerned either with recovering a more natural relationship with their environments or with arriving at a surer sense of identity.

Further evidence of the neo-romantic attitude is found in the character of Cash Bentley, through whom John Cheever presents the problem of the has-been or aging athlete in his short story "O Youth and Beauty!" However, Cheever's sure sense of irony holds this story together, so that Cash's apparently successful outer appearance is sacrificed to the image of the champion track star he longs to retain, with the pathetic result that Cash's life becomes a travesty of his former athletic identity.

In *Rabbit, Run* John Updike's Rabbit Angstrom is a younger version of Cash Bentley. He, too, longs for the meaningful experience of his athletic past, but his passive approach to the realistic demands of life labels him a failure. His worship of self is almost religious in its intensity, but in the case of Rabbit as neo-romantic, we shall see that the traditional image of the sporting hero and his intimate relationship with nature has become inverted. Without ever relishing the sweat and pain of the pursuit, the urban hero's quality of mobility is an agonizing experience.

Perhaps the supreme achievement of the neo-romantic encounter is *The Natural*, in which Bernard Malamud relates the experience of his super-athlete, Roy Hobbs, to the mystical aspects of baseball in order to present the dominant themes of modern literature—the quest for identity, the breakdown in communication, and the failure of love. In Malamud's version of the sporting myth the American Dream can never be realized, but the suffering one undergoes in its pursuit can result in self-knowledge, a far greater accomplishment in Malamud's vision than material gain or fame.

The Death of Innocence: The Paradox of the Dying Athlete

> it seemed clear that wars were not made by generations and their special stupidities, but that wars were made instead by something ignorant in the human heart.
> —John Knowles, *A Separate Peace*

> Dying old is in the cards, and you figure on it, and it happens to everybody, and you are willing to swallow it but why should it happen young to Bruce?
> —Mark Harris, *Bang the Drum Slowly*

The aura of innocence surrounding the traditional figure of the sporting myth is compellingly dramatized through the image of the dying athlete in both John Knowles's *A Separate Peace* (1959) and Mark Harris's *Bang the Drum Slowly* (1956). The predicament of dying young when contrasted with the sporting hero's quest for immortality is strikingly used in these novels to comment on the meaning of individuality in our day. In both works this definition grows out of the interrelationship of their two main characters—that between Gene and Phineas in *A Separate Peace* and Henry Wiggen and Bruce Pearson in *Bang the Drum Slowly*. In both novels, too, the death of one character results in self-knowledge for the other, who in both cases happens to be the narrator. While Gene Forrester gains a fuller understanding of the evil that separates man from man, Henry Wiggen acquires a greater respect for the worth and dignity of the individual.

Essential encounter in *A Separate Peace*, while set against the larger background of World War II, focuses on the minor wars declared among the schoolboys of Devon, a prominent New England preparatory school, in order to explain the larger question of why wars come about. The friendship between Gene and Phineas, two offsetting personalities in that the former is a superior student and the latter an accomplished athlete, is eventually disrupted by what at first appears to be a trifling incident but is later expanded to support the novel's inherent theme: wars are caused by "something ignorant in the human heart."

In schoolboy literature related to the sporting myth, the major conflict exists between the ivory tower and the playing field, or authority and self-expression; thus much of the significance of *A Separate Peace* is projected through the imagery and metaphor of the game. It is appropriate to observe here, too, that because they provide opportunity for self-expression, the playing fields of Devon are equated with the traditional wilderness of the sporting myth. As Gene informs us near the beginning of the novel:

> Beyond the gym and the fields began the woods, our, the Devon School's woods, which in my imagination were the beginning of the great northern forests. I thought that, from the Devon Woods, trees reached in an unbroken, widening corridor so far to the north that no one had ever seen the other end, somewhere up in the far unorganized tips of Canada. We seemed to be playing on the tame fringe of the last and greatest wilderness. I never found out whether this is so and perhaps it is.

The playing field as representative of the forest in microcosm becomes the great, good place, or the "last and greatest wilderness," where the inherent innocence of Phineas can find true expression. As Gene sees it, Finny believed that

> "you always win at sports." This "you" was collective. Everyone always won at sports. . . . Finny never permitted himself to realize that when you won they lost. That would have destroyed the perfect beauty which was sport. Nothing bad ever happened in sports; they were the absolute good.

The game of blitzball, which Finny himself invents to perk up a dull summer at Devon, is more than an example of his ingratiating manner with his fellow students; the game is a symbol of his very being:

> He had unconsciously invented a game which brought his own athletic gifts to their highest pitch. The odds were tremendously against the ball carrier, so that Phineas was driven to exceed himself practically everyday when he carried the ball. To escape the wolf pack which all the other players became he created reverses and deceptions and acts of sheer mass hypnotism which were so extraordinary that they surprised even him; after some of these plays I would notice him chuckling quietly to himself, in a kind of happy disbelief.

Phineas has a Hemingwaylike devotion to enjoyment of sporting endeavor as a thing in itself. His breaking a school swimming record and not reporting his feat for the record emphasize both his uniqueness as an individual and his role as a type of the sporting hero, in that to Phineas the pursuit is more important than the goal. But his athletic accomplishments also add to the fear already present in the inner being of Gene, his roommate, and his best friend. Gene tells himself: "You and Phineas . . . are even in enmity. You are both coldly driving ahead for yourselves along." But the interrelationship of both characters is structured to bring about the novel's tragic denouement and dramatize its basic theme.

As the story develops, Gene's gnawing but unfounded fear that Phineas, out of envy, is seeking to destroy his reputation as a student causes him to mistake Phineas's real intentions. The upshot of this is a betrayal by Gene that results eventually in the death of Phineas but ultimately in the self-education of Gene. The Super Suicide Society of the Summer Session is another one of Finny's improvisations that not only brings out his athletic ability but also further endears himself to his adventure-starved classmates. To become a member of this "secret" organization one must merely leap from a tree limb that hangs treacherously over the river skirting the Devon campus. But Finny, ever the daredevil, proposes that he and Gene jump together. Gene, for some unaccountable reason, which he later explains to Phineas as "just some ignorance inside me, some crazy thing inside me, something blind," jounces the limb, causing Finny to fall to earth and break a leg. Still the innocent, Phineas, even though now physically through with sports, vicariously continues to identify with the sporting encounter through Gene: "Listen, pal, if *I* can't play sports, you're going to play them for me." To which command Gene feels that "I lost part of myself to him then . . . this must have been my purpose from the first: to become a part of Phineas."

If, like another figure in American literature, Phineas becomes a victim of his own innocence, then Gene, through his confrontation with the force of evil, gains self-knowledge at the expense of his own happiness, a state symbolized by his former relationship with Phineas. A dominant theme in our literature, the death of innocence results from the growth of experience. From the time of breaking his leg on, Phineas's existence, both physically and symbolically, becomes a slow death; and as Gene progresses in self-knowledge, Phineas diminishes in force as individual while increasing as image and symbol. A central trait of Gene's makeup is revealed when he says:

> I was used to finding something deadly in things that attracted me; there was always something deadly lurking in anything I wanted, anything I loved. And if it wasn't there, as for example with Phineas, then I put it there myself.

Contrast this outlook with that of Phineas, who, Gene observes, is "a poor deceiver, having had no practice," and in whom there "was no conflict except between athletes, something Greek-inspired and Olympian in which victory would go to whoever was the strongest in body and heart." In becoming a part of Phineas, though, Gene is made more aware of the difference between his own nature and Finny's, of the distinction between good and evil, of the contrast between illusion and reality.

Phineas, then, is the incarnation of the sporting hero before the fall, and in his world of the game there is no reminder of the real war going on in the outside world. When he is training Gene in his place for the '44 Olympics, Finny refutes Gene's observation that there will be no Olympics in 1944 with: "Leave your fantasy life out of this. We're grooming you for the Olympics, pal, in 1944." Phineas's flat denial of a schoolmaster's remark that "Games are all right in their place . . . but all exercise today is aimed of course at the approaching Waterloo" is not only indicative of his natural antipathy toward the authoritarian attitude of the academician, but also exemplifies his philosophy of a world without war or, in effect, a world of Edenic innocence. Perhaps the one activity in the novel that best illustrates Phineas's special genius for maintaining his sense of the way the world should be is his organization of a winter carnival, a kind of comic bacchanal performed in the dead of the New England winter. Because of it, Gene tells us that a "liberation" had been "torn from the gray encroachments of 1943, that an escape had been concocted, this afternoon of momentary, illusory, special and separate peace." In this womanless world of the Devon School for boys, Phineas's outlook asserts that the innocent state can be retained for as long as one can separate self from the man-made or obligatory realities that engulf it. However, Knowles implies that the seeds of discord are inherent in man, and we sense that it is only a matter of time before Finny's ideal world will be destroyed.

Paradoxically, it is Leper Lepellier's departure as "the Devon School's first recruit to World War II" that serves as the catalyst for Gene's encounter with self and prepares the way for the novel's denouement. Leper, viewed as an oddball by his classmates, is a romantic who finds personal identification with the simple realities of nature. Thus he is easily persuaded by a recruiting movie about the ski troops that at least one area of the war experience has its fine moments. However, Leper's sensitivity is undermined by his contact with the military, and after fleeing this alien existence for the security of his Vermont home, he sends for Gene, a friend he believes he can confide in. Now, though, with a more realistic perspective on life, Leper is moved to remind Gene of his evil act: "'You always were a savage underneath. I always knew that only I never admitted it. . . . Like a savage underneath . . . like that time you knocked Finny out of the tree.'" Leper, once an innocent himself, can now recognize evil for what it is, and Gene, although fearful of the truth, in yet another step toward self-awareness must return to Devon and Phineas to discover it for himself. Phineas, still holding onto his "separate peace," reveals to Gene an even more heightened contrast between illusion and reality. As Gene says:

> I found Finny beside the woods playing and fighting—the two were approximately the same thing to him—and I stood there wondering whether things weren't simpler and better at the northern terminus of these woods, a thousand miles due north into the wilderness, somewhere deep into the Arctic, where the peninsula of trees which began at Devon would end at last in an untouched grove of pine, austere and beautiful.

Once again the sporting figure is identified with the primal virtues of the wilderness, and standing on the edge of Finny's snowball fight, Gene is hesitant as to which side to join, his outlook reflecting his present state of being—a Hegelian sense of self-alienation in which a dialectical development controls the individual consciousness and its progress from innocence to maturity. Having become increasingly aware of two antithetical ways of looking at experience, Gene, at this point, can say of his own experience that he no longer needed a "false identity; now I was acquiring, I felt, a sense of my own real authority and worth, I had had many new experiences and I was growing up." Now, "growing up" demands the renunciation of the illusory world of the child, and in terms of Gene's new experience, Phineas and what he stands for must "die." During a secret court in which Gene is placed on trial, the truth of what actually happened in the tree is about to be revealed, but Finny, in one last effort to cling to the significance of his world, rushes from the room, falls down a flight of stairs, and reinjures his leg. Complications set in, and a few days later he is dead.

The death of Phineas is necessary to Gene's experience, because, even though Phineas had thought of Gene as an "extension of himself," Gene's contact with the real facts of existence compels a break with the way of life Phineas represents. As Gene puts it concerning Phineas's funeral: "I could not escape a feeling that this was my own funeral, and you do not cry in that case." The death of innocence—the world of illusion and Edenic reverie—has instilled in Gene a new way of "seeing." After one of his last talks with Phineas, Gene feel that he now has to "cope with something that might be called double vision," since the familiar objects of the campus have taken on a different appearance:

> I saw the gym in the flow of a couple of outside lights near it and I knew of course that it was the Devon gym which I entered every day. It was and it wasn't. There was something innately strange about it, as though there had always been an inner core to the gym which I had never perceived before, quite different from its generally accepted appearance. It seemed to alter moment by moment before my eyes, becoming for brief flashes a totally unknown building with a significance much deeper and far more real than any I had noticed before . . . and under the pale night glow the playing fields swept away from me in slight frosty undulations which bespoke meanings upon meanings, levels of reality I had never suspected before, a kind of thronging and epic grandeur which my superficial eyes and cluttered mind had been blind to before.

Gene's new vision now focuses on complexities where there had formerly been a simple plain of existence equated with the innocent world of sporting endeavor. With the death of Phineas, then, Gene's essential encounter is complete, and at the end of the story he tells us:

> I was ready for the war, now that I no longer had any hatred to contribute to it. My fury was gone, I felt it gone, dried up at the source, withered and lifeless. Phineas had absorbed it and taken it with him, and I was rid of it forever.

Phineas, whose special attitude would have made him a casualty, escapes the disintegrating effect of war, whether it be between individuals or nations, escapes even the fact of losing his basic innocence and growing into a Christian Darling or a Rabbit Angstrom. The "separate peace" declared by Phineas is genuine, for as Gene observes in comparing Phineas with his other classmates:

> Only Phineas never was afraid, only Phineas never hated anyone. Other people experienced this fearful shock somewhere, this sighting of the enemy, and so began an obsessive labor of defense, began to parry the menace they saw facing them by developing a particular frame of mind.

In contrasting two complementary types of the sporting myth, *A Separate Peace* meaningfully dramatizes the dangers involved when the individual

encounters this inner enemy, for it is a powerful and mysterious foe, one that demands a special kind of defense.

Like Phineas, Bruce Pearson of Mark Harris's *Bang the Drum Slowly* is an innocent type, but a Jack Keefe kind of innocent, who apparently commands little respect from his associates and who ironically knows that he is going to die. Unlike other sporting figures, Bruce has little status as a third-string catcher for the New York Mammoths (he is a big-league player however), while the story's narrator, Henry Wiggen, is a starting pitcher for the club. But we shall see that such a relationship is essential to the story's theme. Apparently feeling that Henry is the only person he can confide in, Bruce calls him during the off-season with the news that he is in a hospital in Rochester, Minnesota. Upon his arrival there, Henry discovers that Bruce is suffering from Hodgkin's disease and is given not too long to live, or, as Bruce puts it, "I am doomeded." Henry, who has never really been too friendly with Bruce before (he has strange habits like urinating in hotel washbowls and spitting tobacco juice out of the windows), feels compelled now to take Bruce under his wing. In order that Bruce not be dismissed from the club and may bow out gracefully, Henry resolves not to tell anyone on the team of Bruce's condition during what may be his final season in baseball. It is this special knowledge of Bruce's tragic predicament that bring's about Henry's experience of encounter, for now he begins to observe things and events in a new light. Upon leaving Minnesota for Bruce's home in Georgia, Henry hears the station attendant who puts anti-freeze in their car remark that "this will last you a lifetime." Henry is moved to reflect on this statement:

> You would be surprised if you listen to the number of times a day people tell you something will last a lifetime, or tell you something killed them, or tell you they are dead. "I was simply dead," they say, "He killed me," "I am dying," and more. I don't know if Bruce did. You never know what he notices nor what he sees, nor if he hears, nor what he thinks.

As an innocent, Bruce is seemingly oblivious to the social significance of what goes on around him. His is an instinctive nature that finds itself most at home in familiar surroundings, and the closer they get to Bruce's home near Bainbridge, the more emotionally intense become his recollections of the playing fields of his youth. As Henry puts it, to Bruce "Georgia is a special place, different than all the others"—another reference to the great, good place that seems solidly imbedded in the subconscious of the sporting figure, a place where he "would of give most anything to settle down forever on . . . , never mind the fame and the glory, only give him time to live." Thus, during his stay at home, Bruce is moved to ask Henry a question that has perplexed the philosophers of all ages:

> "tell me why in hell I clumb to the top of the mill a million times and never fell down and killed myself, and why I never drowneded in the river, and why I never died in the war, and why I was never plastered by a truck but come clean through it all and now get this disease?"

It is a question, of course, that Henry cannot answer, but one that gives him an even more sensitive insight into Bruce's plight: "He stood a chance of living a long time yet, not too long but long enough, and I tried to keep him thinking of things yet ahead." If, as usual, the theme of the dying athlete stresses the brevity of life, in this case it also lays emphasis on the unique worth and dignity of the individual. When Henry tells his wife, Holly, of Bruce's situation, he reveals that "she always like him. She always said, 'Add up the number of things about him that you hate and despise, and what is left? Bruce is left.'"

To Henry, the competitive nature of the game of baseball itself reflects the intrinsic worth of any human being, even when he exists as opponent: "'The man you are facing is not a golf ball sitting there waiting for you to bash him. He is a human being, and he is thinking, trying to see through your system and trying to hide his own.'" In answer to Bruce's admission that he has "never been smart," Henry praises those natural instincts of Bruce that distinguish him from other individuals:

> "You been dumb on one count only. You left somebody tell you you were dumb. But you are not. You know which way the rivers run, which I myself do not know. . . .
> "You know what is planted in the fields and you know the make of cows. Who in hell on this whole club knows one cow from the other? I could be stranded in the desert with 412 cows and die of thirst and hunger for all I know about a cow."

Dutch Schnell, the manager of the Mammoths, is aware of something strange about the relationship between Henry and Bruce, and is fearful of what their actions might do to his team's pennant chances. A holdout at the beginning of the season, Henry, before signing, has a clause put into his contract insuring that he and Bruce "will stay with the club together, or else go together." Dutch is determined to get to the bottom of the matter, since he feels that his catching department is weak anyway. In fact, he hates putting Bruce in the lineup, because he always errs in receiving and giving signs. Consequently, Bruce is a kind of nonentity to Dutch, who never "spoke to him when he seen him around. But he carried him along. To him Bruce was a spare part rattling in the trunk that you hardly even remember is there between looks."

In this work, which owes so much to the Mark Twain-Ring Lardner vernacular tradition, Harris has used irony in such a controlled manner that he manages to avoid the pitfall of sentimentality. The drama of the story is heightened by the process of Bruce's slow death's being played out against the background of a championship pennant race, Henry's finest pitching record in several seasons, and Holly's giving birth to Henry's first child. The skillful interweaving of these events creates a poignant situation in which the significance of Bruce Pearson's role and identity is sharpened to its most meaningful extent. The meaning of life takes on more immediacy because of the fact of impending death. It should be noted also that Henry's position as a life insurance salesman during the off-season adds much to the basic framework of the story, where in the beginning he informs us that he has already sold Bruce a $50,000 policy, the kind Henry refers to as "North Pole coverage" because it "covers everything except sunstroke at the North Pole." It is the role of this insurance policy in *Bang the Drum Slowly* that affords us still another example of the strained relationship between sporting figure and woman.

Naïve, and lacking in self-awareness, Bruce has fallen in love with a prostitute name Katie, whom he wants to marry. Katie, who runs a lucrative business at her place, is not interested in marrying someone "dumb from the country," but she is interested in Bruce's insurance policy. Apparently aware of his dying condition, she urges him to change the beneficiary to her name and then she will marry him. Bruce presents her request to Henry a number of times, but Henry, wise to Katie's designs, always manages an excuse. He also successfully wards off Katie's temptations, one of which is a "golden lifetime pass" to her establishment. To Katie's observation that life is short, so "why not live it up a little?" Henry replies:

> "I do not know," I said, and that was true, for I did not. Do not ask me why you do not live it up all the time when dying is just around the corner, but you don't. You would think you would, but you don't. "I do not know why," I said.

Some of the other team members, who have always looked upon Bruce as a fall guy, begin to "rag" him concerning either his "pending" marriage with Katie or his unseemly relationship with Henry. Finally, in an attempt to curtail some of the jokes about Bruce, Henry tells Goose Williams about his condition. Goose is sworn to secrecy, but he tells his roommate, and after Bruce suffers an attack, Henry urges his teammates to let up on him. It is not long before the entire club learns of Bruce's predicament. Their collective attitude at this point is akin to that of Henry's when he condemns his own selfish thoughts:

> When your roomie is libel to die any day on you you do not think about bonus clauses, and that is the truth whether anybody happens to think so or not. Your mind is on *now* if you know what I mean. You might tell yourself 100 times a day, "Everybody dies sooner or later," and that might be true, too, which in fact it is now that I wrote it, but when it is happening sooner instead of later you keep worrying about what you say *now*, and how you act *now*. There is no time to say, "Well, I been a heel all week but I will be better to him beginning Monday" because Monday might never come.

Now painfully aware of one individual's mortality and his role in life, the team begins to recognize Bruce's unique contribution to the success of their pennant drive. Although weak at detecting signs, Bruce is a dependable hitter, and Dutch feels compelled to put him in the lineup for this ability alone. The fact that Bruce is playing a position for which he is not suited (Henry attests to this fact throughout the novel) adds to his functional significance in the story. Furthermore, the juxtaposition of Bruce's plight with the devil-may-care attitude of his replacement, Piney Woods, lends emphasis to yet another irony of life—some individuals taunt the very image of death and still go on living. When he is not playing baseball, Piney gives Dutch gray hairs by driving motorcycles in such reckless fashion that one player remarks, "With all the ways of dying you would think a fellow would wait from them, not go out looking." But near the end of the season death comes looking for Bruce Pearson, and he finishes up on the bench as cadaverous in appearance as the image of the cowboy in Piney's song, parts of which periodically appear in this section of the story:

> O bang the drum slowly and play the fife lowly,
> Play the dead march as they carry me on,
> Put bunches of roses all over my coffin,
> Roses to deaden the clods as they fall.

At the close of the novel, after Henry's having served as a "pallbear" at Bruce's funeral, his eulogy exists as a reminder that his encounter, or education in learning to respect the worth of the individual, is over:

> He was not a bad fellow, no worse than most and probably better than some, and not a bad ballplayer neither when they give him a chance, when they laid off him long enough. From here on in I rag nobody.

It is significant that both narrators of the novels examined in this section grow as individuals through their intimate relationship with the experience of the other, more tragic figures. *Bang the Drum Slowly* is infinitely more than a dirge or eulogy for a fallen sporting hero. It is a humanistic hymn that, in recognizing man's fallibility and mortality, also praises his identity in the common experience of all men.

GORDON E. SLETHAUG

The Play of the Double in A Separate Peace

By Johan Huizinga's account in *Homo Ludens*, play is present in a broad range of cultural activities, including religious observance, poetry, philosophy and organized combat: "The spirit of playful competition is, as a social impulse, older than culture itself and pervades all life like a veritable ferment. Ritual grew up in sacred play; poetry was born in play and nourished on play; music and dancing were pure play. Wisdom and philosophy found expression in words and forms derived from religious contests. The rules of warfare, the conventions of noble living were built up on play-patterns." Later critics such as Roger Caillois and Jacques Ehrmann, however, find this definition too narrow, for one thing because Huizinga retains only one characteristic of play, *agon*, its competitive aspect, whereas another important consideration is *paidia*, spontaneous play. These are two important kinds of play, each with a beginning and end, a magic circle of activity, players, the goal of winning, and certain rules, the violation of which is without question foul play. Through the device of the double, John Knowles in *A Separate Peace* compares two fundamentally different conceptions of the game of life, Gene's which is a great, hostile and crushingly serious *agon* for domination, and Phineas' which is flippantly playful, truly *paidiac*.

Although this handling of play is unique to *A Separate Peace*, the nature

From *The Canadian Review of American Studies* 15, no. 3 (Fall 1984). © 1984 Canadian Association of American Studies.

of the double itself follows customary usage. As Milton F. Foster points out, the book shares a common basis with such works as *The Secret Sharer* and *Heart of Darkness* where the narrator is the main character but where the other character, his *alter ego*, occupies most of his thoughts. This view of the second self as a projection of the protagonist's unconscious is fully elaborated both by Otto Rank and Ralph Tymms who see this phenomenon in Freudian terms as Narcissism. In these works, there is a significant sense in which one character parallels or contrasts with another in a deliberate and obvious way, so that the two are seen to be complementary or warring aspects of a central self or identity. In the romances of Conrad these characters may resemble each other, oftentimes exactly although sometimes in fierce opposition, but in more realistic works such as *The Sun Also Rises, The Great Gatsby* and *A Separate Peace*, these characters (Jake Barnes and Robert Cohn, Gatsby and Nick, Gene and Finny) will not wholly resemble each other physically but will still have enough affinity that there is no mistaking their relationship nor the resultant implied character-ideal projected by the conflict. In this respect, *A Separate Peace* and these predecessors perfectly illustrate Rank's and Carl Keppler's thesis that the significant literature of the double results from a notion of twinship, either the twin as evil persecutor or beneficent savior. But this book carries the issue even further: Gene is the persecuting double, bent upon his own selfish will to power and desired annihilation of Finny, while Finny is the beneficent double, through his sacrificial death bringing about hope and spiritual growth for Gene.

Knowles's purpose in creating this double is to explore two radically different ways of relating with people and coping with an environment. These ways, *agon* and *paidia*, contrast the contestable, competitive attitude and warlike spirit in which the playful is largely absent with a lighthearted, carefree and joyful spirit of play in which the competitive, battling element is sharply reduced. Gene's is the spirit of *agon*, serious rivalry tantamount to war where the spirit of friendliness and play is buried, and Phineas' is the attitude of *paidia*, a generally more ludic vision, where human relations are characterized less by competition and more by the spirit of true joy and unfettered play.

The book's story line is deceptively simple. The narrator, Gene Forrester, and his friend, Phineas (Finny), are both students at Devon, an eastern American private school. The narrator is the more conscientious student of the two, but Phineas is the more gifted athletically and socially. Because Phineas is so well liked and because he seems often to draw Gene away from his studies, the narrator becomes more and more anxious and competitive, finally causing crippling injury to his friend. The book concludes following a kangaroo court session in which Gene is accused of deliberately injuring Finny and after which Finny, rushing from the session, reinjures himself and dies during corrective surgery.

Knowles creates the notion of the double both with respect to the symbolic setting and time of the tale as well as to the characters themselves. The New England setting of the story, the magic circle of the game, is punctuated by the private school and its situation between two rivers, the Devon and the Naguamsett. These two rivers, one pure and fresh, the other ugly, dirty, marshy and salty are divided by a dam. As James Ellis concludes, the Devon suggests Eden, a place for prelapsarian joy and happiness, while the Naguamsett indicates a landscape destroyed by the fall. The school itself stands as a paradox with a double sensibility much like the rivers. Gene describes this sensibility as "opulent sobriety." Although the buildings are unadornedly built of typically New England College red brick and white clapboard shutters, the inside exceeds and undermines the puritan exterior. The inside consists of pink and white marble with heavy ornamentation and crystal chandeliers. The two styles belie one another and suggest radical dissonance. (This dissonance, of course, reflects the notions of games for Gene and Phineas. Gene's is the serious, practical, Puritan view, while Phineas' is the ebullient, baroque and whimsical.)

The time and seasons of the story carry similar connotations of yoked, apparently irreconcilable polarities. Beginning during the lazy summer of 1942 before America was completely geared up and committed to the war, this part of the story stresses the idyllic, peaceful, relaxed and non-conventional school term tragically concluded by Finny's injury that leads into the formal, conventional austere Fall and Winter terms during which the warfront is brought to the fore of everyone's conscious and subconscious life. Consequently, summer and peace are opposed to winter and war, though both are seen as necessary, partially tragic, bondings of opposites. The Second World War where man's competitive games are carried to their most comprehensive and devastating conclusions, is the controlling metaphor of the book. This metaphor, expanded to its fullest, becomes, as James L. McDonald notes, the theme of war, embracing the conflict of nations which results from the conflicts and misunderstandings of individuals such as Gene and Finny that ultimately stem from an unresolved conflict within the self, something primal and ineradicable within every man.

This conflict is best seen through the characters of Gene and Finny, one from the North and one from the South, who are highlighted against the background of Devon. As their friend Leper notes when seeing them together in the tree before Finny's fall, they "looked as black as—as black as death standing up there with this fire burning all around them." At that moment the two stand virtually indistinguishable and harmonious: neither exists independently of the other. In fact, the purpose of their presence in that fatal tree is to take the "double jump," in which the two boys, identical in age, height and build, are to establish a new record by jumping together. To a great extent, the boys have a special intuitive twin-like rapport, and this jump is designed to cement that bond which has been seen before, for instance when Finny intuitively knows that Gene is afraid to jump, and when he openly expresses admiration for Gene's tan while Gene is secretly admiring his.

This quality of the second self knowing what the first is thinking is one of those attributes of the double tradition, for it marks the inexplicable, almost magical sympathy between the two personalities. At this point in the relationship the bonding of the ludic and agonic is still wholesome. Gene's *agon* has not yet grown uncontrollable, though it will shortly do so. The two tend to be viewed as doubles also by their classmates even after the fall and Finny's disabling, as indicated when Gene applies as assistant manager of the team and Quackenbush refers to him as maimed, and after at the kangaroo court when Brinker snidely comments that Finny seems to have Gene's words in his mouth. Together the two could have been strongly supportive, a blending of highly diverse and contrary elements within human nature, but as they stand, the triumphs and achievements of Finny tend to gall Gene, pushing him toward the precipice of catastrophe that typifies the realistic double. Gene sees Finny as a tempter, while the reader sees Gene as the typically malevolent betraying pursuer of the double tradition. An irrational opposition exists between them even as does an irrational attraction. As is typical of the human context, in this fictional world the polarities are not permitted to merge, blend and unite. Rather, they pull apart, largely due to Gene who sees a growing threat in the person of Finny, even while he is attracted to him and held by their friendship. It is Finny in fact through whom Gene comes to define and understand himself.

The spirit of *paidia*, Phineas is described as a green-eyed, five foot eight and one half inch athletic youth who balances "on one foot on the prow of a canoe like a river god, his . . . body a complex set of balances and compensations, each muscle aligned in perfection with all the others . . . his whole body hanging between river and sky as though he had transcended gravity and might by gently pushing upward with his foot glide a little way higher and remain suspended in space, encompassing all the glory of the summer and offering it to the sky." His combined good looks, fine sense of balance and tremendous energy create the sense of an adamic, unfallen youth or some Dionysus whose physical beauty predates and transcends his twentieth-century context and whose playful attitude has not been corrupted by any negative spirit of competition. His athletic triumphs reinforce this picture, for without much exertion Finny manages to take several prizes for football, hockey and other bodily-contact sports. In one especially telling instance, he swims the pool with only Gene present, earning a better time than the champion swimmer but refusing to divulge the results for public acclaim or to repeat the incident in front of others. He does things for himself, not for public approval and congratulation. In effect, he has no spirit of competition; he simply tests himself within the rules of the game and performs as well as he can. For him the game itself is in most respects his opposing player. He has no particular wish to compete with and win over another person.

When Finny feels that the rules of the game need to be abandoned or changed, he does so with delight for he is not one to be tied to unnecessary and inconsequential rules: he is "a student who combined a calm ignorance of the rules with a winning urge to be good, who seemed to love the school truly and deeply, and never more than when he was breaking the regulations, a model boy who was most comfortable in the truant's corner." In this way he is, as Clair Rosenfield points out, the "good-bad boy" in the sentimental American tradition. When he bends or breaks the rules and shows his unconventionality, he does so with no animosity and so wins others to his opinion, no matter how outrageous the occasion. Only he can with impunity skip dinner after dinner or sleep at the beach when he should be in his room studying. Only he can wear a pink shirt in 1942 and not be called a fairy. And only he can wear the Devon school tie incorrectly as a belt and not be punished by the headmaster. He is equally imaginative and successful in creating his own games and rules. In effect, as the spirit of play, his mind is continually inventive, thinking up new games which will serve as amusement and joy for others. It is he who thinks up the game of Blitzball and the rules for jumping from the trees. Finny is also the one who, even after his leg has been splintered, invents the winter carnival, a sort of boys' school Mardi Gras where invention and chaos take primacy over convention and order. Finny is the spirit of playful inventiveness and freedom from circumscribing rules.

Finny's manic quality extends into every corner of his personality and life. His seemingly careless abandonment of the rules results from a fundamentally spontaneous, antic, Hellenistic nature which is not limited or distorted by sharply defined intellectual or moral prescription. He feels and enjoys without holding his emotions in reserve or fearing the social repercussions of his gaiety. Quite naturally in the midst of his joy, he tells Gene of his affection for him, to which the narrator admits: "It was a courageous thing to say. Exposing a sincere emotion nakedly like that at the Devon School was the next thing to suicide. I should have told him then that he was my best friend also and rounded off what he had said. I started to; I nearly did. But something held me back. Perhaps I was stopped by that level of feeling, deeper than thought, which contains the truth." Gene's level of feeling, deeper than thought, is agonistic, founded on personal antagonism and even subconscious dislike. Finny's level of feeling, deeper than thought, is one of complete *jeu de vivre*, love and support, whatever the occasion: when Gene lashes out at him for interfering with his studies, Finny is most gracious in backing off; when Gene almost falls out of the tree, Finny risks saving him; when it becomes clear to Finny that Gene has pushed him from the tree, Finny is deeply hurt but ultimately forgiving. His sense of play is morally and physically uplifting for him and others.

Although Finny's self-expression is instinctual and uninhibited by social rules or intellectual restrictions, he is neither morally unconscious nor ignorant. He does nothing dishonest, and he does not lie, never intending deliberately to deceive people or to make himself look good. What may in certain instances seem deceptive is mere playfulness and gamesmanship. Even his declaration that there is no war in Europe is less a stubborn refusal to see reality than a means of sustaining a group joke and snubbing his nose at a war that is radically changing his environment from one of youthful innocence and sportiveness to one of adult experience and cynicism. Of course, his refusal to admit the war into his sphere of reality is also, as he says, a means of protecting his feelings: he desperately wants to participate in this heroic enterprise but is refused because of his splintered leg. Rather than growing negative and bitter, self-accusing and accusing of others, he playfully says there is no war and by that means buoys up his own spirit as well as his classmates'. In short, Finny is an exquisite, unique, prelapsarian youth with "an extra vigor, a heightened confidence in himself, a serene capacity for affection. . . . Nothing as he was growing up at home, nothing at Devon, nothing even about the war had broken his harmonious and natural unity. So [the narrator adds] at last I had." The narrator's tribute to Finny is truly touching, capturing as it does the "liberation we had torn from the gray encroachments of 1943, the escape we had concocted, [the] . . . momentary, illusory, special and separate peace." Finny encapsulates all that is best and highest in youth, all that is possible when filled with the sense of the ludic, and Gene with his guilt-ridden knowledge of having destroyed him represents the tragic vision of conflict that opposes the playful one of comedy and peace.

Although Finny calls Gene his best friend, Gene is unable to return the compliment despite his later coming to realize the inherent value of the relationship. But until just before Finny's death, Gene cannot let go of his opposition to Finny. With his distinctly Spartan sensibility, he *must* see everything as *agon*, as a competition to the death. Finny and Gene are much alike, but at the same time they are polar opposites as much as the Devon and the Naguamsett are physically or as much as Summer differs from Winter. Although the book centers first on Finny (Gene is not even named for the first twenty-seven pages), the reader is always interested in Gene's reaction to Finny because Gene is the narrator and because he obviously has changing reactions to his friend, ranging from love and adulation to envy, mistrust and hate. Of the same height and build as Finny, Gene can wear his clothing. But unlike Finny, Gene is not especially athletic and mistrusts himself and others in sports. He maintains, "I didn't trust myself in them, and I didn't trust anyone else. It was as though football players were really bent on crushing the life out of each other, as though boxers were in combat to the death, as though even a tennis ball might turn into a bullet." For him harmless sports become harmful combats, tennis balls turning into bullets, *paidia* into *agon*.

Consequently, Gene initially considers himself capable of serving only as an assistant team manager, though when Finny later trains him he seems capable of something better. Similarly, he does not have the energy and endurance of Finny and tends to be fearful of jumping out of the tree until Finny shames him into it, fearful of missing dinner or spending an illegal night on the beach, and fearful of dropping an examination. Gene's laurels are not garnered in the world of sports but in academia where he aims to be the best in the class, not just a good student, but an exceptional one. He puts his mind to this task in a cynical way, knowing that his rival, Chet Douglass, is "weakened by the very genuineness of his interest in learning." Gene has no genuine interest in learning but only in becoming the head of the class; his is a single-minded, competitive spirit where he aims not to improve himself and his mind or to test himself against the subject matter, but rather to pit himself against all oncomers, all academic contestants, and to defeat them, to crush the life out of them. Gene lives by his intellect, by his rational side, with the edge of competition sharply honed to keep him in isolation.

Gene feels this competition and rivalry to be quintessential Devon. He notices those instincts in himself, and he attributes them to others as well. So, he aims at being head of the class because he assumes that Finny aims at being the best athlete in order to subvert Gene's own triumph. Early in the summer of '42 he comes to this "realization": "I found it. I found a single sustaining thought. The thought was, You and Phineas are even already. You are even in enmity. You are both coldly driving ahead for yourselves alone. You did hate him for breaking that school swimming record, but so what? He hated you for getting an A in every course but one last term. You would have had an A in that one except for him. Except for him." Furthermore, he says of Finny: ". . . I had detected that Finny's was a den of lonely, selfish ambition. He was no better than I was, no matter who won all the contests." Contrary to what Gene believes or wishes to admit, what he discloses in these thoughts is not Finny's competitive nature but his own because he is a youth who sees everything as competition and rivalry and everyone as an enemy striving to win a battle.

Because Gene regards everyone as a rival or an enemy, he maintains even fifteen years later that "The war was and is reality for me. I still instinctively live and think in its atmosphere." To some extent, Gene's pushing Finny off the branch, setting in motion the circumstances leading to Finny's death, is integrally tied to his own view of life as war. Guiltily, he notes: "I never killed anybody [in the Second World War] and I never developed an intense hatred for the enemy. Because my war ended before I ever put on a uniform; I was on active duty all my time at school; I killed my enemy there." Because Gene perceives his classmates as enemies, he adopts the secretive cunning of a fighter who feels that the game of life does not consist of right or wrong but of the vanquishers and the vanquished, the winners and the losers. He believes that "The thing to be was careful and self-preserving."

He will lie implicitly or explicitly to preserve his image; so, he puts pictures above his bed which will lead people to believe that he is landed gentry from the deep South; and when he is put on trial at the kangaroo court, he lies about not being in the tree when Finny fell so that his crime will not be discovered. He also has a kind of animal cunning which allows him to think that, because Leper has become psychotic and has been given a dishonorable discharge from the war, his testimony against Gene will not be believed by his classmates. Of course, he is wrong about that one, but the incident still illustrates the devious, circumlocutional quality of his mind and morality. Leper, in fact sees right through him when he remarks: "You always were a lord of the manor, weren't you? A swell guy, except when the chips were down. You always were a savage underneath."

Gene finally wants to win so badly that he will violate the rules of the game, undermining and even abolishing the game element. Civilized play gives way to savage carnage. Huizinga has noticed that the truly agonistic often borders on meanness, and will, in certain instances, subvert the joy of the game: "Tension and uncertainty as to the outcome increase enormously when the antithetical element becomes really agonistic in the play of groups. The passion to win sometimes threatens to obliterate the levity proper to a game." Since Gene understands so little about *paidia*, the spirit of play, the idea of winning supersedes his respect for the skill and honor of playing and winning or losing by the rules. As a result, he engages in several forms of combat which are considered non-paideiac and non-agonistic and which, ultimately, subvert the game: "The surprise, the ambush, the raid, the punitive expedition and wholesale extermination." For him playful competition gives way to a lust for power.

Given his attitude to life as agonistic conflict, ultimately war itself, and his view of ethics as survival tactics, Gene's mode of operation at Devon and his undermining of Finny are characteristic. He is fearful of authorities and does not wish to challenge their rules directly, nor does he wish to lose face with his comrades. He does not want others to know that he is subverting the game's rules, even the game itself. As a result, he often feels caught in a dilemma, caught between supporting the established rules and saving face with Finny who cares little about rules. When faced with that dilemma, he inwardly resents Finny and does his best to subvert him. Even when Finny saves him from falling out of the tree, he is at first thankful and then scornful, first praising and then blaming him. Because Gene cannot learn openness, cannot back away from his rationalized, protective view of life, his jealousy and resentment of Finny grow. Instead of being a "harmonious and natural unity" as is Finny, he becomes fragmented and unnatural. When that unnaturalness and fragmentation intensify, Gene must destroy Finny by pushing him out of the tree; Finny is his rival double that must be destroyed.

The act of pushing Finny has two direct consequences: it makes a cripple of Finny, forcing him to reassess his view of life; and it subjects Gene to a considerable amount of guilt and a new perception of himself in relation to Finny. Physically, Finny's fall is tragic but necessarily human, as was Adam's in eating the fruit or Donatello's of Hawthorne's *Marble Faun* in murdering the model. But the difference in these falls is that Finny is not responsible for his own whereas Adam and Donatello were. Nevertheless, in all cases a new standard of behavior is imposed and a world view revised. Finny is, of course, physically harmed by the fall, his leg splintered in such a way that he cannot participate in sports. His sphere of play is sharply circumscribed. Still, his attitude is, for the most part, one of cheerful optimism. He does not blame Gene, and he continues to laugh and joke.

At certain times, however, he shows a growing negative sensitivity to his wounding; he acknowledges that he now understands the world and human motivation (the fat old men who organize the war) because he has suffered. And some of his jokes have a cynical, cutting edge: there is no war for him because he is crippled and cannot be accepted into the military. Yet, he does not fully suffer until he realizes the extent of Gene's conscious betrayal of him, until he realizes that Gene viewed him as an enemy and pushed him from the tree out of hate, until he realizes that Gene has wantonly destroyed the very game itself. When he comes to the painful awareness that Gene wanted to hurt him, he almost despairs, but Gene's confession to him brings him around once again to an acceptance of their friendship and life, to his belief in the continuing beneficence of their game and friendship. Finny can come to this acceptance because he himself bears no guilt.

Gene, however, comes to bear a hideous sense of shame as a result of breaking the understood rules of the game, try as he may to suppress that fact. Initially, he manages to conceal from himself the implications of his act. He forgets that Leper had watched him push Finny, and he does not consciously assimilate the fact that Leper has withdrawn from him. Nor does he fully realize the extent to which his classmates blame and mistrust him, though he is certainly given a strong indication in the Butt Room. Not until Leper goes away, escaping from the military, and Gene visits him, does Gene realize Leper's resentment about his responsibility. Gene, however, strangely rationalizes his role in Finny's fall and begins to feel that he has in some way taken the place of Finny. He becomes the overreacher who tries to destroy Finny out of the game and attempts to serve as a stand-in. He tries to play two roles simultaneously.

Consequently, it is hardly accidental that, after maiming Finny, Gene begins to wear his clothing, even his pink shirt. He remarks with satisfaction: "when I looked in the mirror it was no remote aristocrat I had become, no character out of daydreams. I was Phineas, Phineas to the life. I even had his humorous expression in my face, his sharp, optimistic awareness. I had no idea why this gave me such intense relief, but it seemed, standing there in Finny's triumphant shirt, that I would never stumble through the confusions of my own character again." Gene now thinks of himself as truly aristocratic and complete, as having altogether usurped the role of, and therefore destroyed, his opponent. Gene even affects the athletic aspirations of Finny, thinking, " . . . I lost part of myself to him then [when Finny says Gene has to play sports now that he cannot], and a soaring sense of freedom revealed that this must have been my purpose from the first: to become a part of Phineas." To their "joint double amazement," Gene shows promise as an athlete when trained by Finny. He even starts to resemble Finny's grimacing when irritated. And at Finny's funeral, Gene thinks of it as his own, admitting to himself that what Finny felt, knew and understood has somehow become what Gene now feels, knows and understands. A clutching, grasping player, he dominates and absorbs his friend, so that he can alone survive this game.

Finally, however, Gene puts things into better perspective. How long that takes is uncertain, but he has achieved that new perspective sometime between his graduation and his return to Devon fifteen years after the accident. During that time, his perception, the way in which he sees reality, especially himself, has undergone a great transition. By that time, he knows how complementary he and Finny were, and also how much his guilt has transmuted the full horror of his deed into something relatively worthwhile. Finny's fall from the tree has symbolically become Gene's fall from grace, his entry into the world of pain and suffering from which he can escape only by guilt and expiation. As a result of his breaking the rules of one game, another, more difficult game is introduced.

Initially, Gene refuses to accept all the implications of his deed. It is true that he tries to tell Finny of his guilt, but when Finny thinks of Gene as momentarily crazed, Gene does not dispute that position and suppresses his guilt. This guilt remains suppressed until the time of the kangaroo court when it is dredged up and finally confronted. Ironically, the motto over the building in which the trial takes place is the Latin inscription for "Here Boys Come to be Made Men." Here, too, another game begins, the trial itself in which Gene finds himself opposing the rest of the class. On this occasion Gene must finally surrender his pretenses and lies, placing himself fully within the confines of this new game, becoming honest with himself and Finny, so that Finny can finally accept Gene's private apology to him and his statement that he belongs with Finny, his veiled statement of love. When Gene can admit that there is something deadly in his love for everything, something for which he alone can be held responsible, then he can begin to profit morally and spiritually from his fall, his own *Felix Culpa*.

With that admission, the hell that he has been experiencing and the game that he has been playing—represented so aptly by the winter weather that "paralyzed the railroad yards"—and the unseemliness of the Butt Room and the kangaroo court, begin to abate. He comes to learn that "feeling becomes stronger than thought," that his relationship with Finny could have been based not upon rivalry but playfulness and instinctual love, and that the conflict between the opposing forces or doubles might have been resolved. As he says on coming back to Devon: "Everything at Devon slowly changed and slowly harmonized with what had gone before. So it was logical to hope that since the buildings and the Deans and the curriculum could achieve this, I could achieve, perhaps unknowingly already had achieved, this growth and harmony myself." At this time in Gene's life, he seems to have reconciled his past with the attributes that make up his personality—though the reader must still remember that Gene does say that for him life is still a war, agonistic conflict projected to a universal level.

What Gene must finally understand—and in this respect his knowledge is deeper and more profound than Finny's who for a long time locked out awareness of Gene's deceitfulness and guilt—is that the root of his hate, the root of the rivalry and competition so prevalent in Devon, and the root of the war which to him represents America, is in fact "something ignorant in the human heart." And that ignorance has nothing to do with the lack of knowledge or intelligence but with some intrinsically selfish quality that willfully destroys such games of peace and innocence as Finny and Devon contained in the summer of '42. With that understanding, Gene may be able to reach out to others in the way Finny did; he may be able to show love; he may be able to establish fidelity and trust; he may be able to play with honesty the games of human relationships; he may be able to work toward balance and harmony in order to bring the double aspects of the human being into alignment. But, as Jake Barnes qualifies of Brett's optimistic statement about the possibility of their love at the end of *The Sun Also Rises*: "Isn't it pretty to think so?"

Unfortunately, we do not see this new possibility put into practice after that fifteen-year hiatus between the end of school and Gene's return. Finny is dead, so the peace that Gene achieves will of necessity be a separate peace. He is apart from the conflict of the human heart, but, tragically, he cannot share that peace with the one whose death brought it into existence. And he may not be able to share that understanding with anyone else. Insofar as he recognizes Finny's worth and insofar as he takes the blame on his own shoulders, there is hope that the narrator of *A Separate Peace* has in fact achieved a lasting peace which he can share with others, a peace which replaces war-like competition and so brings *paidia* and *agon* together. The perception itself may be illumination enough to bring about the hoped for understanding and change.

Chronology

1926   John Knowles born in Fairmont, West Virginia on September 16, the third child of James Myron and Mary Beatrice Shea Knowles.

1942   Enters Phillips Exeter Academy in New Hampshire as a "lower middler" (tenth grader).

1943   Attends a summer wartime session at Phillips Exeter called the Anticipatory Program; is a member of a group called the Suicide Society where members jump from a tree into a nearby river.

1944–46   Graduates from Phillips Exeter in August 1944. Enters Yale University for fall 1944 term before enlisting in the U.S. Army Air Force. Spends eight months in aviation cadet training program before being discharged from the service in 1945. Returns to Yale in 1946.

1947   Begins submitting short stories to the *Yale Record*.

1948   Begins working for the undergraduate publication the Yale *Daily*; is elected to *Daily*'s editorial staff

1949   Graduates from Yale with a bachelor's degree in English.

1950–52   Becomes a reporter and drama critic for the *Hartford Courant* in Connecticut.

1952–56   Tours England, Italy, and France; writes first novel, titled
           Descent to Proselito. The novel is accepted for publication but
           Thornton Wilder advises Knowles to withdraw it. Moves to
           New York and becomes a freelance journalist; begins
           contributing to *Holiday* magazine.

1953   First story, "A Turn in the Sun," is published in *Story Magazine.*

1956   *Cosmopolitan* publishes the short story "Phineas," which contains
           the basis for *A Separate Peace.*

1956–60   Joins the staff of *Holiday;* moves to Philadelphia. Begins work on
           A Separate Peace.

1959   *A Separate Peace* is published in Great Britain; receives favorable
           reviews.

1960   Macmillan publishes first American edition of *A Separate Peace*
           in February to critical acclaim; novel wins the Rosenthal Award
           from the National Institute of Arts and Letters and the William
           Faulkner Award for the most promising first novel of the year. It
           is also nominated for the National Book Award. Knowles
           resigns from *Holiday* to devote himself to fiction writing and
           travel; visits the Middle East and Greece.

1962   Publishes second novel, *Morning in Antibes,* based on his visit to
           the Riviera; the book earns mostly negative reviews.

1963–64   Serves as writer-in-residence at the University of North
           Carolina at Chapel Hill.

1964   Publishes *Double Vision: American Thoughts Abroad,* a collection
           of travel essays.

1966   Third novel, *Indian Summer,* is published; Knowles dedicates
           the novel to his mentor, Thornton Wilder. The book becomes a
           Literary Guild Selection.

1968–69   Serves as writer-in-residence at Princeton University; publishes
           short story collection, *Phineas: Six Stories.*

1971   *The Paragon,* Knowles's fourth novel, is published.

1972   Film version of *A Separate Peace* is released.

1974   Fifth novel, *Spreading Fires,* is published.

1978   *A Vein of Riches,* a novel about the coal-mining business in West
           Virginia, is published.

1981   *Peace Breaks Out*, a companion novel to *A Separate Peace* that is also set at the Devon School, is published.

1983   *A Stolen Past*, a novel set at Knowles's alma mater, is published.

1986   *The Private Life of Axie Reed* is published.

1999   At work on autobiography; resides in Florida.

Contributors

HAROLD BLOOM is Sterling Professor of the Humanities at Yale University and Henry W. and Albert A. Berg Professor of English at the New York University Graduate School. He is the author of over 20 books, including *The Anxiety of Influence* (1973), which sets forth Professor Bloom's provocative theory of the literary relationships between the great writers and their predecessors. His most recent book, *Shakespeare: The Invention of the Human* (1998), was a finalist for the 1998 National Book Award. Professor Bloom is a 1985 MacArthur Foundation Award recipient, served as the Charles Eliot Norton Professor of Poetry at Harvard University in 1987–88, and has received honorary degrees from the universities of Rome and Bologna. In 1999, Professor Bloom received the prestigious American Academy of Arts and Letters Gold Medal for Criticism.

JAMES ELLIS is emeritus professor of English at the University of North Carolina at Greensboro.

JAY L. HALIO is a professor of Shakespeare and modern fiction at the University of Delaware. He has held two Fulbright-Hays lectureships, and from 1985 to 1997 was chairman of the editorial board of the University of Delaware Press. He is the author of more than 20 books, mostly on Shakespeare, and has edited editions of *King Lear*, *Macbeth*, *The Merchant of Venice*, and *Henry VIII*.

RONALD WEBER received his Ph.D. from the University of Minnesota. He has been a professor of American Studies at the University of Notre Dame since 1963.

PAUL WITHERINGTON is a professor of English at the University of the Pacific in Stockton, California.

JAMES M. MELLARD is a professor at Northern Illinois University. He also serves on the editorial board of *Mississippi Quarterly*.

FRANZISKA LYNNE GREILING teaches high school English at Highland Park High School in Michigan.

JAMES L. McDONALD is a professor of English at the University of Detroit Mercy.

PETER WOLFE is the author of numerous works on literary figures, including *Craft and Vision in William Gaddis* (1999), *Alarms and Epitaphs: The Art of Eric Ambler* (1993), and *The Disciplined Heart: Iris Murdoch and Her Novels* (1966).

IAN KENNEDY taught at Southwest Missouri State University and received his Master's degree in English from the University of Virginia. He has also written for the *Arizona Quarterly*.

WILEY LEE UMPHLETT has a Ph.D. in literature from Florida State University. He is editor and author of several books and numerous articles on sports, American culture, and literature, including *Achievement of American Sport Literature: A Critical Appraisal* (1991) and *Creating the Big Game: John W. Heisman and the Invention of American Football* (1992).

GORDON E. SLETHAUG is a professor of English at the University of Hong Kong, specializing in American literature with emphasis on the American Renaissance and the contemporary novel and film.

Bibliography

Bryant, Hallman B. *A Separate Peace: The War Within.* Boston: Twayne Publishers, 1990.

———. "Finny's Pink Shirt." *Notes on Contemporary Literature* 15 (1984): 5–7.

———. "Symbolic Names in Knowles's *A Separate Peace.*" *Names* 34 (1986): 83–88.

Carragher, Bernard. "There Really Was a Super Suicide Society." *New York Times* 8 October 1972, sec. 2, pp. 2, 7, 17.

Ellis, James. "*A Separate Peace:* The Fall from Grace." *English Journal* 53 (1964): 313–18.

Foster, M. P. "Levels of Meaning in *A Separate Peace.*" *English Record* 18 (1968): 34–40.

Halio, Jay. "John Knowles's Short Novels." *Studies in Short Fiction* 1 (1964): 107–12.

Haniz, Linda, and Roy Huss. "*A Separate Peace:* Filming the War Within." *Literature Film Quarterly* 3 (1975): 160–71.

Knowles, John. "A Special Time, A Special School." *Exeter Bulletin* (Summer 1995): 1–4.

McDonald, James L. "The Novels of John Knowles." *Arizona Quarterly* 23 (1967): 335–42.

McDonald, Walter R. "Heroes Never Learn Irony in *A Separate Peace.*" *Iowa English Bulletin Yearbook* 22 (1972): 33–36.

Mengeling, Marvin E. "*A Separate Peace:* Meaning and Myth." *English Journal* 58 (1969): 1323–29.

Powell, David L. "John Knowles." *Contemporary Novelists.* London: St. James Press, 1976.

Travis, Mildred. "Mirror Images in *A Separate Peace and Cat and Mouse.*" *Notes on Contemporary Literature* 5 (1975): 12–15.

Ward, Hayden. "The Arnoldian Situation in *A Separate Peace*." *Bulletin of West Virginia Association of College English* 1 (1974): 2–10.

Witherington, Paul. "*A Separate Peace:* A Study in Structural Ambiguity." *English Journal* 54 (1965): 795–800.

Wolfe, Peter. "The Impact of Knowles's *A Separate Peace*." *University Review* 36 (1970): 189–98.

Acknowledgments

"*A Separate Peace:* The Fall from Innocence" by James Ellis. From *The English Journal* 53, no. 5 (May 1964): 313–18. © 1964 National Council of Teachers of English. Reprinted by permission.

"John Knowles's Short Novels" by Jay L. Halio. From *Studies in Short Fiction* 1, no. 2 (Winter 1964): 107–12. © 1964 Newberry College. Reprinted by permission.

"Narrative Method in *A Separate Peace*" by Ronald Weber. From *Studies in Short Fiction* 3, no. 1 (Fall 1965): 63–72. © 1965 Newberry College. Reprinted by permission.

"*A Separate Peace:* A Study in Structural Ambiguity" by Paul Witherington. From *English Journal* 54, no. 9 (December 1965): 795–800. © 1965 National Council of Teachers of English. Reprinted by permission.

"Counterpoint and 'Double Vision' in *A Separate Peace*" by James M. Mellard. From *Studies in Short Fiction* 4, no. 1 (Fall 1966): 127–134. © 1966 Newberry College. Reprinted by permission.

"The Theme of Freedom in *A Separate Peace*" by Franziska Lynne Greiling. From *English Journal* 56, no. 9 (December 1967): 1269–1272. © 1967 National Council of Teachers of English. Reprinted by permission.

"The Novels of John Knowles" by James L. McDonald. From *Arizona Quarterly* (Winter 1967): 335–42. © 1967 *Arizona Quarterly*. Reprinted by permission.

"The Impact of Knowles's *A Separate Peace*" by Peter Wolfe. From *The University Review* 36, no. 3 (March 1970): 189–198. © 1970 The Curators of the University of Missouri. Reprinted by permission.

"Dual Perspective Narrative and the Character of Phineas in *A Separate Peace*" by Ian Kennedy. From *Studies in Short Fiction* 11, no. 4 (Fall 1974): 353–59. © 1974 Newberry College. Reprinted by permission.

"The Neo-Romantic Encounter" by Wiley Lee Umphlett. From *The Sporting Myth and the American Experience*. © 1975 by Associated University Presses. Reprinted by permission.

The Play of the Double in *A Separate Peace*" by Gordon E. Slethaug. From *The Canadian Review of American Studies* 15, no. 3 (Fall 1984): 259–270. © 1984 Canadian Association of American Studies. Reprinted by permission.

Index